Start a Cupcake Business Today:

InformationTree Press
Middlebury VT, USA

Edited by Paula Spencer

ISBN: 978-0-9816469-1-6

Printed in the United States of America

Acknowledgements:

The editors at Information Tree Press would like to extend our sincere gratitude to our copy editor Jenny Rankin for her keen eye and red pen. Without her diligent effort, this book would still be a work-in-progress.

Contents

INTRODUCTION.. 5

EDUCATION...11

PLANNING FOR SUCCESS 20

THE FINANCIAL PLAN................................61

DEVELOPING YOUR BRAND...........................71

LEGAL CONSIDERATIONS................................98

LOCATION, LOCATION, LOCATION.......................... 113

FOOD SAFETY 128

INGREDIENTS FOR SUCCESS 132

EXPENSES 138

MANAGING YOUR BUSINESS 145

MENU PLANNING.............................. 157

AVOIDING MISTAKES 163

GROWING YOUR BUSINESS.......................... 170

APPENDIX 175

1

INTRODUCTION

As a baker looking to turn your skill and passion into a dream business, you're probably reading this book because you are interested in finding out what it takes to start this fun, hip and highly profitable business.

The passion for all things cupcake has exploded since the late 1990's and shows no sign of slowing down. The craze that began with New York City's Magnolia Bakery and immortalized on *Sex and the City* spawned an industry. Cupcake shops have opened up in every major U.S. city and many smaller ones as well. Customers can find cupcakes online, via catalogues, at farmers markets, from mobile vending trucks, kiosks, major restaurant chains, home bakers and more. While some predicted the cupcake market would reach a saturation point or that the economic collapse that began in 2008 would be the end of the cupcake trend, the demand is still growing.

This business has so many positive attributes. Your products will bring a range of emotion – joy, pleasure, nostalgia – to so many people and will often be at the center of your customers' celebrations. You get to unleash your creativity and develop not only a delicious, handmade product but also a brand experience that reflects your own personality and contribution to this worldwide phenomenon. As a business owner you will become a vital member of your community. Both your customers and those with whom your cupcakes are shared will appreciate the high quality ingredients, custom flavors, and unique pleasure that comes from a cupcake bakery.

There's also a very enticing, lifestyle changing, profit potential. As popular as the cupcake phenomenon has become, there is still a growing demand for new shops, providers and niches within the market. Two of the target consumers for cupcakes -- food aficionados, who are eager to find and share new culinary experiences, and brides, who prefer cupcakes to traditional wedding cake, are perpetual opportunities. Cupcakes are prefect for birthdays (everyone has one), bridal or baby showers, corporate events or almost any type of gathering. Likewise there are millions of customers who would love to indulge in a delicious cupcake after lunch, dinner or during an afternoon lull, but find it challenging to locate freshly baked items in their neighborhood. With very few major national competitors operating in the United States, the sales opportunities for local operations are virtually limitless. Even with our recent economic troubles, people are still spending money on small indulgences, especially bakery items.

This confection captures the essence of many contemporary conditions: a resurgent interest in crafting, a nostalgia for simple childhood pleasures, the slow food movement, the increased awareness and availability of premium handmade foods and ingredients, and more. We as consumers love to splurge on small things.

As communities across the U.S. and worldwide look to recover from the economic damage of the last few years, many places will see a surge in small business efforts -- individual entrepreneurs who recognize that building a vibrant community requires unique flavor and experiences easily distinguished from the massive homogeneous chain stores. This movement away from big box stores toward small, sustainable and locally produced products is easily witnessed in the baking industry. The impact has been an increase in revenues in the U.S. bakery industry to more than $34 billion annually, according to Frost & Sullivan.

While bakery sales have always been strong in the U.S.—according to *Food Safety Magazine*, the average American eats 53 pounds of bread, 119 pounds of cereal and 14 pounds of pasta each year and about 35,000 cookies in his or her lifetime—there is not much chance that the bakery industry will die off any time soon. Niche operations such as cupcake bakeries are perfectly positioned to take advantage of this food trend.

Perhaps you've been told by friends and family that you should go into business for yourself because of the scrumptious treats you make for holiday and birthday celebrations. Perhaps it's simply been your dream to provide delectable desserts to the people in your community and be involved with the special events that occur in people's lives. Whatever your reason, opening a cupcake business takes a great deal of time, planning, dedication, and commitment.

While the bakery industry as a whole continues to thrive, individual businesses come and go very quickly, often not surviving the first year. This book has been designed to provide you with the most up-to-date information possible to help ensure your success, giving you the tools and education which, when partnered with your motivation, business savvy, and a tasty product, will help you rise above the competition.

Bakery Trends

It used to be commonplace for every community to have at least one "mom and pop" bakery where consumers shopped for all of their bread goods such as cakes, dinner rolls, Italian bread for pasta night, desserts, etc. In the last twenty years, grocery store chains Walmart, Costco and others have moved into these markets and have driven many full-service bakers out of business. Even before the economic crisis of 2008, a bakery decline was occurring for the last decade, driven in large part to increased competition in the full-service arena.

Smart entrepreneurs have adapted and responded to the market conditions by developing specialty niches that consumers seek. Cupcakes are just one niche within this market. Their rediscovery is due in part to the popularity of reality television shows featuring cakes and cupcakes.

Trends that have emerged throughout the food industry such as premium ingredients, internationally influenced flavors and the slow food movement are creating a new breed of bakeries. Growth areas include:

Health
- organic
- heart-healthy (trans fats are out)
- farm-fresh
- allergen-free (gluten-free, vegan)

Global Awareness
- fair trade (chocolate)
- international and layering of exotic flavors
- green (locally-produced)

Lifestyle
- quick and convenient (mobile vending)
- indulgent : premium gourmet
- grazing: unique treats offered by small operations conveniently located

INTRODUCTION

One of the strongest trends in the specialty food industry as a whole is an increased awareness of our health, our planet and our society. This trend has emerged from the green movement, the slow food movement, and the resurgence of health awareness. Increasingly, people relate the food – even the desserts – that they consume, to their environmental commitment and their desire to be good citizens of the world. Supporting local farms and local businesses supports this philosophy. For others, buying from a business that creates from scratch, in small batches and with premium ingredients means better taste and better health.

Gourmet and artisanal bakeries often enjoy a perception of being healthy and green. Organic, fair-trade, locally sourced and sustainable remain important buzzwords to consumers. While it is important to understand the perceptions in your own community before committing to any concept, don't hesitate to explore different ideas in initial market testing.

There are many things that must be considered when contemplating your cupcake business. Everything from what flavors you will offer to where you will be located to how you will price your cupcakes are all important details you need to begin working out before you open your business.

In fact, the first several chapters of this book are designed to help you through the decisions and steps you should be taking before buying your first ingredient. Just like having the right recipe can mean the difference between a great cupcake and one that no one wants to eat, taking the right steps before you open your business can ensure that you will still be there in the years to come.

Most small businesses fail to thrive, not because they aren't great ideas with the potential for profit, but because the person opening the business did not realize how much work, capital, and planning were required to make the business a success. You can make a profitable, enjoyable boutique cupcake business that thrives in your community with the right planning and resources.

2

EDUCATION

This book is written for the hands-on entrepreneur – someone with a dream and the desire to work in the day-to-day operation of a cupcake business. In any food-service business two of the most important aspects of the operation are product creation and the management of the business. Most people who start bakeries from the ground up aren't business people; they're what The *E-Myth* author Michael E. Gerber calls "technicians" (i.e. people with a skill). For example, someone who loves to make pies and wants to reap the profits of their skill. If your bakery is to survive, you need both technical skills and business skills. The first key to success is to recognize where you need help and seek further education.

Let's start with the technical role: the baker. What are the qualifications to be a baker or pastry chef in a retail operation? Many entrepreneurs have started successful bakeries with little or no formal training; however, it is important for you or someone on staff to have a core set of competencies to run this business. The following self-assessment

11

should help you understand if you need further experience or training.

Communication

☐ Do you communicate effectively with others?

☐ Are you good at problem solving, asking questions to seek advice and clarifying information?

☐ Could you write workplace manuals or procedures to train employees and standardize the business?

☐ Do you have a strong attention to detail?

Team Building

☐ Do you have experience as a leader?

☐ Can you build teams by setting and evaluating goals?

☐ Can you motivate people to complete tasks as defined by you, on time and to your standards?

Mathematical Concepts

☐ Are you able to make estimates of routine workplace measures such as weights, temperatures, and times?

EDUCATION

☐ Are you able to use basic arithmetic processes?

☐ Are you able to notice mathematical errors and provide calculations to make corrections?

Food Safety

☐ Are you familiar with basic food safety practices for personnel, clothing and equipment?

☐ Have you completed food handlers training?

☐ Can you maintain work area in a clean and orderly state to meet health department standards?

Product Sourcing

☐ Are you comfortable locating and negotiating with vendors to supply ingredients?

☐ Are you able to recognize quality and fair prices when sourcing products?

☐ Are you able to identify products that do not meet quality requirements and rectify supply chain errors?

Customer Interaction

☐ Are you an outgoing person and a good listener?

☐ Are you able to interact with customers in a professional, courteous manner; handle complaints sensitively and with discretion; and take follow-up action as necessary to ensure customer satisfaction?

☐ Are you good at recognizing verbal and non-verbal cues to interpret someone's needs or concerns?

Functional Tasks

☐ Do you know how to use a computer? Point-of-sale equipment? Cash Register? Accounting software?

☐ Are you comfortable explaining computer applications to others? Could you install software, operate a website and interact with vendors and customers online?

☐ Can you lift heavy ingredients, work in extreme hot or cold conditions and maneuver safely in a potentially hazardous environment?

☐ Are you able to clean and sanitize equipment to meet health code requirements, prepare equipment for operation after cleaning, and keep accurate records of your process?

☐ Have you ever prepared and managed a large event (catering, large orders, etc.)?

Production

EDUCATION

☐ Do you know how to measure supplies to confirm enough ingredients are available to meet recipe requirements?

☐ Can you develop processes to streamline cupcake production?

☐ Do you have experience creating uniform batches?

☐ Can you operate ovens simultaneously to meet required output, ensure baked product meets food safety and quality requirements?

☐ Are you able to analyze a product to determine the cause of unacceptable product quality?

☐ Do you have experience with cupcake and/or cake decorating; chocolate tempering; preparing fillings; frosting/icing techniques?

☐ Are you familiar with estimating production needs based on demand?

Business

☐ Do you have experience balancing a register/terminal?

☐ Are you comfortable managing/counting cash, checks and credit receipts in accordance with proper bookkeeping procedures?

☐ Do you have experience in processing sales; completing customer order forms, invoices and receipts; identifying and accurately processing customer delivery requirements?

☐ Do you have product development experience? Can you research opportunities for new products by identifying market characteristics and matching opportunities?

☐ Do you understand how to adapt an existing recipe to produce a new product, determine the method of assembly and presentation, and estimate the cost of production?

☐ Do you have experience managing a budget? Forecasting supply requirements?

Answering these questions is merely a guide to help you identify skills in which you may require further experience. If you are confident in all but the business skills, then you are already on the right track by reading this book. There are also many good accounting books geared toward food-service management that explain in great detail how this type of business can succeed. In fact, there is an entire consulting profession geared toward the number crunching of bakeries and cake shops. At the beginning stage, however, most entrepreneurs need the fundamentals and much of the accounting, forecasting, budgeting and inventory management can be learned relatively quickly. Some of these responsibilities can be outsourced to professionals.

Of course, hiring someone to run the "business" part of your business is not an option. Your success depends on understanding the big picture. Too often, bakers, cake decorators and hobbyists consider the artistry of the production the point at which their management ends. Unfortunately, these artists often end up losing sight of the financial condition of the business and eventually fail due to mismanagement. Moreover, as the leader, if you are making decisions based on guesswork, inaccurate assumptions and poor planning, then you will find it difficult to gain the confidence of those around you.

If you found most of your answers to be affirmative for the business-related questions but you don't have the cupcake skills, then you may need more experience baking and decorating cupcakes. Again, just as you can hire a professional to do any job, you are less likely to get the best from your employees if you are not an active participant or can't recognize errors. It is human nature for an employee to have greater respect for someone who has mastered the task that they are being asked to carry out. More importantly, your business is a living entity that should change and grow over time. Your ability to duplicate any process -- whether a recipe or a sales technique -- depends on your ability to document and share it with your team.

You must have enough knowledge of each of your recipes and routines to record them in an operations manual. Without a written record of every process in your business, you can't teach others and the business can't operate in your absence. Many sample documents that are included in an operations manual can be found at our website in the download section. www.cupcake-business/resources.

If your self-evaluation indicates you need greater baking and bakery management knowledge, then the next step is deciding how to prepare yourself.

Culinary school or on-the-job training?

The choice to pursue formal education versus real-life experience is truly a personal one. A big part of the decision is your current skill level as many of the professional schools assume a certain level of knowledge and emphasize advanced techniques, while a bakery owner will employ you as a dishwasher at first, if you have no baking experience. Secondly, you must have a sense of what you ultimately want to get out of the time spent training yourself. Are you seeking a practical education, learned by working from the bottom up or are you passionate about the fine details of the science, culture and history of baked goods?

Working in a bakery will teach you the day-to-day tasks, the stress of customer and financial demands, the interaction with customers, the business processes and the lifestyle that you only gain on the job. However, without some previous kitchen experience, you will most likely find yourself in a role that has little to do with your ultimate objective, such as janitorial work.

A hybrid of combining culinary school with on-the-job training may be the best approach. There is much to be learned and exposed to in both environments and each role enhances the other. Learning the techniques in an academic situation gives you the credibility to approach a bakery for the type of job you want. You can learn the best practices (both culinary and business) while applying that knowledge in a situation with real world repercussions. Since a bakery is your ultimate goal, your curriculum should include not only bread and pastry, but also nutrition, management, marketing and more.

The biggest drawback to pursuing a Culinary School Education is the cost. As an entrepreneur, you will need resources to start your bakery and school can be very expensive.

A third option is to educate yourself by practicing every skill you want to master; reading books, networking with other bakers and pastry chefs and getting experience anywhere you can. This might include volunteering, working in a school kitchen, job shadowing and working for family and friends. There are countless stories of food entrepreneurs who started by sharing their product with those around them, and then growing into full-fledged businesses. Your personal path has everything to do with your current experience and level of passion for filling in the gaps of your knowledge.

PLANNING FOR SUCCESS

The Business Plan

To succeed in any business, not just a cupcake business, the first step is writing the business plan. This is not just notes and ideas scribbled on napkins as you dream about the idea of owning your own business, but the concrete, formally written blueprint to your success. In the process of writing your business plan, you will be forced to answer in-depth questions about your motivation, your purpose, and even your competition.

Creating your business plan requires you to think deeply about the type of cupcake business you are planning to create and forces you to consider all of the things that failing small businesses don't consider until they're in danger of going out of business.

Creating your business plan should be something you do *before* you open your business. It not only ensures that you will have a map that helps guide you through the initial decisions of opening your business, but it also enables you to share your vision with others including investors and financial institutions. Without a sound business plan you will be unable to receive either commercial loans or Small Business Association (SBA) backed financing, which are important when you consider that one convection oven can cost around $12,000. A business plan confirms your understanding and analysis of the financial picture, competitive landscape, market prospects, and overall strengths and weaknesses of your proposed business.

Your business plan will consist of a narrative statement, an executive summary, and several financial worksheets. When creating your business plan, the executive summary, which appears at the beginning of the plan document, should actually be written last, as it is only after you've worked through the process of creating your plan that you can adequately summarize the details of your business.

It is a myth that if you are not seeking outside investment, you don't need a business plan. The real value of creating a business plan is not just in having the finished product in hand; rather, the value lies in the process of researching and thinking about your business in a systematic way. It takes you out of the daydream stage of thinking about recipes and happy customers and forces you to think about what really matters—the sound operation of your business.

The act of planning forces you to conduct research and look at your ideas critically. It takes time now, but avoids costly, perhaps disastrous, mistakes later. Ideally, you will discover both holes and opportunities in your current thinking. If you develop your numbers honestly and conservatively, the plan has the potential to highlight cash flow problems. Likewise, a thorough competitive analysis can show you how to capitalize on qualities that only you have and prepare for areas where you need help.

The business plan in the appendix of this book is a hypothetical model suitable as a guideline. However, you should modify it to suit your particular circumstances, whether you plan to be a small brick-and-mortar cupcake business, a home-based mail/web order shop, or a delivery-only start-up.

If you are creating a plan to show investors, pay particular attention to your writing style. You will be judged by the quality and appearance of your work as well as by your ideas. Keep in mind that the time most people will take to read your business plan is very limited. Your writing needs to be detailed enough to prove that you know what you're talking about, but succinct enough to get to the point quickly and keep a reader's interest.

It typically takes several weeks to complete a good plan. Most of that time is not spent writing the plan but conducting research and re-thinking your ideas and assumptions. But then, that's the value of the process, so make time to do the job properly. Along the way, be sure to keep detailed notes on your sources of information and on the assumptions underlying your financial data.

If you've never written a business plan, it might feel overwhelming at first. The key is to move through it one section at a time and seek assistance for the parts for which you don't have the expertise or information. Start with some of the easy parts first. If you get hung up on a particular part of the plan--skip it for now--and come back and fill it in later. Don't worry about making a perfect first draft--just get some thoughts down to get the process going and you can always come back and polish it up later.

Before you start the plan, do some research in your community. Make sure you have considered the requirements for success:

Need Does your community need the kind of cupcake business you want to create? The research indicates that the need is growing, but if there are already bakeries in your community, how can you profit from an underserved niche? Would a different location be more competitive?

Customers Are you thinking local or global? Are there enough potential local customers who will be interested in your treats? If not, what will you need to do to reach the rest of the world? If so, how much will you have to spend on advertising to reach your local clients? Can your community afford your ideal vision or do you need to scale back?

Location Will it be conveniently located? Can you afford the rent in a higher visibility area?

Products Do you know what your prospective clients want? (An upscale, gourmet cupcake, a gluten-free alternative, etc.) Can you produce a product your customers want, at a price they want to pay and still make a profit?

Once you have answered the above success requirements, you will have a sense of the kind of thinking that goes into a business plan. The following chapter presents a high-level overview of what you can expect in each part and some of the research you will need to conduct as you work on your plan. Remember, you don't have to write a plan in any specific order and your local SCORE office is happy to help you with your plan [http://www.score.org] SCORE provides free online and face-to-face business counseling, mentoring, and training.

Elements of a Business Plan

A typical business plan has about 10 sections. Parts 1-4 describe your business and your product. Emphasize the elements of your cupcake business that will distinguish you from the competition and your particular skills and expertise. Talk about the market you are targeting and provide factual, non-hyped details for why this audience will buy from you. Explain what stage of development your business is in.

Section 1

1.1 Cover page

While seemingly obvious, a cover page is an important first impression that shows the reader, at a glance, the nature of the business and the professionalism of the author(s). Be sure to include the Business Name, your logo (if available) or a picture of your cupcakes and all of your contact information including your name, phone number, email address and website (if complete).

1.2. **Table of Contents**

The table of contents is simply a list based on the headings of each section and subsection in the body of your document. It is important because it gives a quick overview of the scope of the plan and enables readers to navigate quickly to specific areas of interest. A banker for example, may skip past the narrative parts of the plan, and go directly to the financials. An investor may only have an interest in the executive summary.

A Table of Contents can also be used to plan the document before you even start writing. You can lay out the document in advance to build the skeleton of what you want the document to be. This does not mean you should complete the document in the order of the list or that the layout cannot change and grow. It is simply a good idea to know the framework of the business plan rather than assembling something hodgepodge at the end.

1.3. **Basic Information**

You should provide a list of all of the basics of your cupcake business – The owners, partners, their addresses and contact information; business structure; professional advisers such as accountant, attorney, banking contacts

1.4. Introduction

This is a brief narrative that introduces the business to which the rest of the plan refers. The intro should explain the purpose of the plan as a planning tool and fund raising vehicle. Briefly introduce the author and the layout of the plan.

2. Summary

A summary highlights the key points you want readers to take away. If a reader only has time to read a single page of your plan, imagine the importance of this section. This summary should comprise your complete business on a single page of 4-5 paragraphs. It is written after the plan has been drafted because you don't know what to summarize until you have written it. This section should be succinct -- about two pages or 10 % of the total plan in length. Additionally it should paint a positive, yet realistic picture. For some readers the summary is the sales pitch and will determine if further reading is of interest. Be sure to give this section plenty of time.

3. Business Description

While it might seem obvious to you, explain what business you will be in and what you will sell. Begin with a general description in a single sentence such as: "Gourmet, vegan cupcakes made from the finest locally-sourced ingredients."

You might include:

3.1. A Mission Statement

Do you offer something unique and consider it your mission to bring it to market? (e.g. organic or gluten-free)

3.2. Company Goals and Objectives

Explain why you want to be in business. This statement should reflect the underlying reasons for running your cupcake business. These objectives could cover growth, profitability, offerings and markets. Objectives are shorter-term markers along the way to goal achievement. For example, a goal might be a successful franchise operation of your initial cupcake concept in 5 years. The objectives might be annual sales targets and some specific measures of customer satisfaction.

3.3 Business Philosophy

What is important to you about running a cupcake business?

3.4 Overview of your market and the cupcake industry.

What changes are on the horizon (long-term and short-term) and how do you plan to prepare and capitalize on them?

3.5 Strengths and Core Competencies

What factors will make the company succeed? What do you think your major competitive strengths will be? What background experience, skills, and strengths do you personally bring to this new venture?

3.6 Legal form of ownership

Sole proprietor, Partnership, Corporation, Limited liability corporation (LLC) and why you have selected this form (See Chapter 6: Legal Considerations).

4 Products and Services

In this section, you will describe your cupcakes. You can list all of the individual flavors you sell or you might describe the pricing structure of the different sizes or combinations and a general pricing structure for whole-sale vs. retail sales. This is a great opportunity to think about pricing.

PLANNING FOR SUCCESS

Basic Questions to consider:

- What benefits do your cupcakes provide and what position or image do you want to convey?
- How broad will your product line be?
- What new products or flavors will you introduce?
- What brand concept will you try to develop or reinforce?
- What will be your pricing strategies? (For example: premium, indulgent, local)
- Why will customers pay your price?
- What will be your credit policies be for wholesale clients?

4.1 **Pricing**

Outline your proposed pricing plan for each cupcake variation (e.g. full size, mini, minimum orders, etc.) If you plan to do catering or wedding towers, think about the different types of pricing models. Use simple tables and put any detailed pricelist or menu in the appendix.

4.2 **Competitive Analysis**

What bakeries and other businesses/products will compete with you?

First, identify how many bakeries selling cupcakes in your market area. Then, identify those that appeal to the types of customers that you plan to serve. You should also identify all other bakeries located in your immediate area even if they don't sell cupcakes, because they can also influence your business. Consider including grocery stores, farmers markets, delis, etc. Refer to the Yellow Pages or websites like Yelp.com for listings of area bakeries.

It is important to identify any bakeries, especially cupcake-selling shops, that have closed, and for what reasons. Also, learn what new bakeries are planned in your proposed community and determine how they might affect your operation. If you plan to sell online, identify those cupcake businesses as well as mail-order companies. (Our website has a full listing.)

After identifying your competition, visit and evaluate the ones (at least two) that you sense will be your greatest competition. Speak with the manager of these operations if possible. Use the following checklist to take notes for your analysis.

Location
Community traffic patterns
Proximity to sources of demand
Accessibility
Visibility
Surrounding neighborhood
Parking availability
Sign visibility

Appearance/Comfort
Exterior appearance and theme
Interior appearance and theme
Atmosphere
Cleanliness
Heating and ventilation

Menu
Theme
Variety and selection
Signature items
Price range and value
Beverage choices

Cupcake Quality
Taste
Presentation
Portion size
Consistency

Service
Days open
Hours of operation
Service style

Quality of service
Speed of Service
Friendliness

General Information
Number of seats
Types of guests served (age, income, origin...)
Is business increasing or decreasing?
Catering offered?
Entertainment
Franchise affiliation
Reviews by food Critics / Ratings in travel guides, Yelp
Local reputation
Advertising and promotion methods used
Website quality

Overall
Strengths
Weaknesses

With your notes, create a competitive analysis comparison table. This table will include columns for each of your competitors, yourself and the above competitive factors. You will rate your competitors and yourself from 1 to 5 (1 = weak; 5 = strong). Try to be very honest here. A competitive analysis can be very informative. You should discover areas in which you are weak and areas in which you can capitalize on the failings of your competitors. And remember that you cannot be all things to all people. In fact, trying to be causes many bakeries to lack a concept in the customer's eye.

In the final column, estimate the importance of each competitive factor to the customer: 5 = critical; 1 = not very important. Use this number to weigh the scores more accurately by multiplying it by the individual scores. Scoring higher on the factors that customers most care about obviously outweighs poor scores on the less critical factors.

After completing the graph, write a short paragraph stating your competitive advantages and disadvantages. Understanding your strengths and weaknesses will help you carve out your niche. Use the analysis to guide your niche strategy. A sample competitive analysis chart is provided in the appendix and at our website.

5. **Customer Profile**

This is a very important, though sometimes ignored section. Allow plenty of space to identify your targeted customers, their characteristics, and their geographic locations (otherwise known as their demographics). While this data can be very challenging for a start-up cupcake business owner to acquire, it is important that the research be clear, specific and authentic. This information will convey if there really is a sustainable demand. If you plan on wholesale clients in addition to your retail operation you should also analyze this demographic.

You may have more than one customer group. Identify the most important ones. For example, you may want to consider the difference between the customers who buy from you during the weekday and those that shop on weekends. If you have a farmer's market presence, then think about the difference for each customer group and construct a demographic profile. Do this for each major group of customers. Include the following:

- Age
- Gender
- Location

- Income level
- Social class and occupation
- Education
- Other (specific to your industry)
- Other (specific to your industry)

For business customers, the demographic factors might be:

- Industry (such as restaurant or caterer)
- Location
- Size of business and buying potential
- Price and product preferences

One way to convey the potential value for wholesale clients such as restaurants is to quantify these customers within your community and estimate the value of their business. For example if there are 100 restaurants in your surrounding region what is the most likely number that will do business with you? What is the theoretical value of a single contract (e.g. 120 cupcakes per week) over a year? What is the growth potential as you ramp up your operation and can meet more business demand? You may find that wholesale margins are too slim compared to selling directly to your own customers until you have greater scale.

There are two kinds of market research: primary and secondary.

Primary research means gathering your own data. For example, you could use the yellow pages to identify competitors, and do surveys or focus-group interviews to learn about consumer preferences. A traffic count is another data point you can research yourself if you are opening a retail operation. You simply go to the location you're considering and count the cars that pass. Typically you count the cars that pass on the same side as the location, for an hour in the morning, at noon, and during evening rush hour. Average the traffic to approximate the daily numbers. How about foot traffic? Often the local chamber of commerce, or even the landlord will have these numbers. Professional market research can be very costly, but there are many books that show small business owners how to conduct effective research themselves.

Secondary research means using published information such as industry profiles, trade journals, newspapers, magazines, census data, and demographic profiles. This type of information is available in public libraries, industry associations, chambers of commerce, from vendors who sell to your industry, and from government agencies. ZipSkinny (http://zipskinny.com) and FedStats [fedstats.gov] can provide some initial demographic information. Demographic maps can also be purchased. [http://www.buydemographics.com] These maps provide detailed population estimates, the current and predicted number of households, families, median age, and median household income. These numbers will help you project the size and income of your target audience. You should also consider purchasing a "Retail Goods and Services Expenditures" map for your community, as this will tell you how much people in your proposed location spend on bakery goods in a year. Obviously, it is advantageous to locate your shop in an area where household income and food expenditure is higher. These maps are eye-opening and well worth the minimal investment.

Start with your local library. Most librarians are pleased to guide you through their business data collection. You will be amazed at what is there. There are more online sources than you could possibly use. Your chamber of commerce has good information on the local area. Bakery trade associations and trade publications often have excellent data geared toward the bakery industry in general. You will have to make some assumptions for cupcake-specific business information. (See Appendix for a list of trade associations and publications.)

In your marketing plan, be as specific as possible; give statistics, numbers, and sources. The marketing plan will be the basis, later on, of the all-important sales projection. Most importantly, remember that conducting research should not only be done sitting behind your computer. This step requires you to go out into the world, look around at your community, talk to others and gather information.

6. Marketing, sales and projections

No matter how good your cupcakes are, your business cannot succeed without effective marketing. You should have already uncovered much information about your target market. Use the business planning process as your opportunity to consider the best ways to reach them. Indicate very specifically in this section the tactics you will use to introduce your cupcake business and bring customers through your doors. If you are selling online, what methods will you use to advertise your bakery? Facebook? Twitter? Have you identified low-cost methods to get the most out of your promotional budget?

Will you use methods other than paid advertising, such as word-of-mouth (How will you stimulate it?) free press, and social networking?

What image do you want to project? How do you want customers to see you? In addition to advertising, what plans do you have for graphic image support? This includes things like logo design, cards and letterhead, brochures, signage, and interior design (if customers come to your place of business).

Should you have a system to identify repeat customers and then systematically contact them on Facebook and Twitter?

Promotional Budget

How much will you spend on the items listed above? What is the promotion strategy before start-up? (These numbers will go into your start-up budget.) How much will you spend on marketing monthly? (These numbers will go into your operating plan budget.)

7. Management Team

It is important for anyone reading your business plan to know your qualifications as well as the structure of your new business. If you do not have extensive business experience do not inflate this area. Rather, be honest about your background and focus on your passion for all things cupcake. More importantly, if your plan reflects a lack of business experience, then you should seek trusted advisors who can guide you. This may be a relative or friend who may be an unpaid consultant. The main thing is to have someone you can reach out to when you have questions.

8. Operations.

This section describes how you will produce your cupcakes. You should include details that estimate the production process timeline and quantity of goods you will make each day. Any key supplier relationships such as bulk ingredients or paper goods supplier should be identified here. How will you get your items to wholesale vendors? If you are selling online, how will you ship? How will you keep products fresh?

Basic Questions for this section
- How and where are your cupcakes produced?
- What is the capacity of your baking set-up and can you produce enough cupcakes to meet sales goals?
- Do you have any specialized production techniques or recipes? If so, are there any associated costs?
- How will you insure quality control?

- What is your customer service policy / approach?
- How much raw ingredient inventory will you keep?
- How will you manage it?
- What qualities do you need in a location? Describe the type of location you'll have.

Physical requirements
- Amount (sq. footage) of space. Include a floor plan if possible to the Addendum.
- Type of building.
- Zoning. Confirm that your proposed location is properly zoned.
- Power and other utilities. Does the current configuration meet your needs?

Cost:
Estimate your occupation expenses, including rent, but also including maintenance, utilities, insurance, and initial remodeling costs to make the space suit your needs. These numbers will become part of your financial plan. What will be your business hours?

8.1 Legal Environment
Describe the following:
- Licensing and inspection requirements
- Permits
- Health, workplace, environmental regulations
- Zoning or building code requirements
- Insurance coverage

8.2 Suppliers
Identify key suppliers:
- Names and addresses
- Type and amount of inventory furnished
- Credit and delivery policies
- History and reliability

Should you have more than one supplier for critical items (as a backup)?

Are there occasions or times of the year, such as the holidays where shortages could be a problem?

Are the costs of basic ingredients such as eggs, flour, chocolate, etc. steady or fluctuating? If suddenly any one of your primary ingredients was in shortage, how would you deal with changing costs?

9. Personnel

The success of many small bakeries depends on their ability to recruit, train and retain employees. Given that many cupcake businesses are small operations, at first this area may not have much emphasis. It should not be ignored however as readers of your plan will want to know you are thinking about the future. Even if you are a one-person operation now, at some point if your business grows, you will need employees.

Basic Questions for this section:
- What are the staff needs now? In the future?
- What skills must they have? What training will you provide?
- Are the people you need available?
- What is their compensation?

10. References

Here, you identify your professional service providers including your accountant, insurance agent, lawyer and your local bank manager. It is also beneficial to list any professional consultants or advisors familiar with your business. Don't worry if you don't have each of these relationships figured out yet. Come back to this (and every) section as you make final decisions.

11. Financial Projections

PLANNING FOR SUCCESS

You must create some financial projections that will give you and anyone looking at your plan a snapshot of the future financial health of your business. This may seem impossible if you don't have any previous records of what to expect. That is why it is so important! You must thoughtfully and honestly assess future cash flows.

Part of your business plan will include the financial numbers you already have and/or the forecasts for the future. You will undertake some research for this part. You will include the following:

- [ ] Sales Forecast and Strategy
- [ ] (Projected) Pro Forma Income Statement
- [ ] Break-even Analysis
- [ ] Projected Cash Flow
- [ ] Projected Balance Sheet

Forecasting helps you allocate your resources (including start-up cash), handle unforeseen complications, and make good business decisions. Because it provides specific and organized information about your cupcake business and how you will repay borrowed money, a good business plan is a crucial part of any loan application. Additionally, it informs suppliers and others about your requirements and goals. Finally, beyond the descriptions you provide, the financial data will help prove the viability of your bakery. You have to make the numbers work to show that what you are planning will, in time, break even and profit. For example, some people begin broadly by estimating the goals they hope to achieve in order to maintain a certain lifestyle and pay off a loan. Others start with the goal of breaking even and plan for increased profits over time.

Often, a new entrepreneur will have a vision for a cupcake business and then find a location or commercial kitchen for rent. Armed with the monthly rent as a baseline expense, she will then start her research for all of the other expenses such as utilities, insurance, build-out costs, equipment, ingredients, etc. While this is important data, it is critical to look at the sales strategy and revenue projections that you can realistically expect from your community.

The financial aspect of starting a business, for most people, is very complicated and therefore avoided. Unfortunately, this leads to magical thinking about money – the ideal that you will concentrate on making great cupcakes and that so much money will come in that cash flow won't be a problem for you. This rarely holds true, so it is important to understand the basics.

The budgets and financial projections of your business plan will convey to potential investors that you not only understand but also are planning for paying your bills and driving your businesses toward profitability. It will also provide a realistic baseline of what to expect for your personal finances. This section should be completed honestly and conservatively, as experienced business people will be examining these numbers carefully. A complete set of spreadsheets and worksheets is provided on our website to help you.

Sales Forecast and Strategy

For your business plan to be convincing, you have to provide a realistic sales forecast. In fact, this forecast is the single most critical piece of information in the plan because it indicates the likelihood for success. Moreover, the sales forecast is used in other areas of the plan such as cash flow projections and budgets. For example, if you think you will sell 300 cupcakes a day, you might need a far different oven, staff, marketing plan and inventory setup than if you estimated 100 cupcakes per day. Is selling 300 cupcakes a day realistic for the kind of business you're planning? Are you planning a smaller or larger business?

If you averaged 300 cupcake sales a day, that could add up to over $270,000 in annual revenue. Of course, you have to have the strategy in place to reach those numbers, the cash flow to meet the expenses, the infrastructure to make and sell that many cupcakes and the customer base desiring your product. Forecasting is kind of like juggling all of those different requirements and assumptions at once. You will find yourself playing with the numbers to the point where the goals seem achievable and the revenue acceptable. If the data points to a satisfactory profit that fits with your personal financial situation and repays any outside investors, then the business plan is working.

Unfortunately, if you don't have any previous sales data to rely on, it is much more difficult to estimate. An informed, legitimate sales forecast can be created from some assumptions about the market in which your business will operate, the competition, the cupcake trends seen in comparable cities, the spending patterns locally, and e-commerce trends if you will sell online. One way to ensure your estimates are accurate, and perceived as credible, is to provide documentation and back-up your numbers with hard data. Of course, if you've been thinking about a cupcake business for a while now, you've seen the success in many locations and the growth in demand. The consumer acceptance of $3.00 cupcakes is proven in many locations and the rapid growth in their popularity, despite a struggling national economy since 2008, is a strong indicator for potential sales in almost any market.

One way to determine sales in your community is to network with bakeries in comparable communities (as they are not in competition with you). You can often find sales figures online for bakeries that are for sale and use those numbers to extrapolate your own figures as a starting point. (bizbuysell.com) Another technique is to estimate sales potential of a geographic target area based on the target customer you are after. For example, if you open your cupcake shop in an area that will have walk-in customers, you should learn about the ebb and flow of traffic during different times of the day. Talk with potential customers about their dessert buying habits, conduct interviews during different times of the day and across several blocks of the proposed location.

Your customer profile research from Section Five will provide the demographic data (population estimates, the current and predicted number of households, families, median age, and median household income) and can help you estimate the size of the marketplace. If you look at the size of the customer base and their consumption habits you can also make some estimations on what percentage of those customers will buy from you. The investment in professional demographic maps is well worth it.

You can also conduct some very simple and useful test marketing at farmers markets with little expense and no risk. Finally, if you have difficulty obtaining sales figures directly, you can try several secondary sources of information. Many suppliers have very sophisticated computer modeling to estimate how much inventory a bakery of your proposed scale would require. They can help estimate your market based on what they are providing other bakeries. You might also try to talk to former employees of the competition or closed businesses. Of course the national trade associations will have some guidelines to share with you as a member and finally you can hire an experienced consultant to help set realistic goals.

Table 1 shows a hypothetical sales forecast for a cupcake shop in a metropolitan area adjacent to a large university campus and retail shopping district. Note that the average direct unit cost of each cupcake is $0.85. Learning how to calculate this number is critical and is covered later in the chapter.

Unit Sales

Your sales projections will be your best guest based on your research as discussed above. You can do this projection multiple times with different scenarios such as best-case, worst-case, etc., based on your understanding of the economic climate, the perceived demand in your community, and the competition you will have.

Direct Unit Cost or COGS (cost of goods sold)
The cost of goods sold will be determined by costing your recipes. For beverages, research the wholesale price of the items you will sell.

Table 1. Sample Sales Forecast Cupcake and Beverages

Sales Forecast	
Unit Sales	
Cupcakes	79,200
Beverages	39,600
Total Unit Sales	**118,800**
Unit Prices	
Cupcakes	$3.00
Beverages	$2.00
Sales Revenue	
Cupcakes	$237,600
Beverages	$79,200
Total Sales Revenue	$316,800
Direct Unit Cost (COGS)	
Cupcakes	$.85
Beverages	$.50
Direct Cost of Sales	
Cupcakes	$67,300
Beverages	$19,800
Subtotal Direct Costs of Sales	**$87, 100**

Once you have an estimate of sales, you can begin to articulate some other parts of the plan and make some high level assumptions about expenses and profits.

Start Up Budget

You will have many expenses before you even begin operating your business. The start-up budget is used to determine how much money will be needed to start your cupcake business and keep it operating until you make a profit. Since businesses do not always make a profit the first year (or more), money is needed to keep the operation going until enough money is generated to cover all the expenses. The start-up budget can be used to determine how much money you will need to start your business.

It's important to estimate these expenses accurately and then to plan where you will get sufficient capital. Most business owners who open retail operations will tell you that arriving at the point where the first cupcake could be sold was much more costly than they anticipated. There are two ways to make allowances for surprise expenses. The first is to overestimate the actual cost of each item in the budget. The problem with that approach, however, is that it destroys the accuracy of your carefully researched numbers. The best approach is to add a separate line item, called "contingencies," to account for the unforeseeable expenses such as a broken air conditioner, a donation to the local street festival, a new grease trap, etc. A rule of thumb is that contingencies should equal at least 20% of the total of all other start-up expenses.

What are my start-up costs?

To start a brick and mortar operation, you need to have first and foremost, a location, equipment and furnishings, utilities (electricity, water, HVAC), someone to do the work (you), and products to sell.

42

Start-up costs also include installation of fixtures and equipment, deposits for public utilities, licenses and permits, accounting and legal services, and business insurance.

A special start-up cost is the start-up inventory. This is the dollar amount for the raw ingredients you purchase to sell to your customers as cupcakes and it is an ongoing expense.

To completely equip a cupcake bakery, the purchase of furnishings for the entryway, restrooms, dining room (if applicable), kitchen, storage, office, and employee areas must be included. The concept (design, brand, theme) should be carried through in everything you do.

Table 2 shows typical start-up costs for a shop with dining space. These numbers are hypothetical as much of your business expense depends on the scale of your business and your sales goals. The operating expenses projected for the first three months of operation are listed as "Suggested Operating Capital," which means the amount of cash you will need in addition to the start up funds to run the business for three months. Ideally, you should have enough cash for six months, taking into account contingencies such as slower times of the year.

Table 2: Cupcake Shop Start-Up Budget

Item	Ex. 1	Ex. 2
Rent (Sec. Deposit & 1st month $1,500 + $1,500)	3,000	10,000
Initial Inventory/ingredients	2,000	11,000
Equipment/Fixtures	10,000	50,000
Improvements and Build-out	5,000	18,500
Licenses, Tax Deposits and Permits	300	500
Utilities Deposit	150	300
Employees	0	7,500
Grand Opening Advertising	500	3,000
Legal Services	150	800
Accounting	100	1,000

Insurance	1,000	3,000
Loan Fees	0	2,000
Incorporation	100	500
Signage	500	10,000
Misc.	500	1,000
Total Costs	23,300	119,100
Suggested Operating Capital	18,900	40,000
Total	**42,200**	**159,100**

Use this chart as a guide. Notice that Example 1 has only $5,000 allocated for build out. This would be an ideal (and rare) situation where a great space was available and required very little to bring it to code or if you offer little/no dining space. These numbers must be realistic and documented. You can look online for equipment costs, call prospective service providers, and use online forums to talk to other business owners about many of these estimates.

One technique for discerning prices in your area is to talk to non-competitive parallel business such as a bread bakery or ice-cream shop. They can give you advice without feeling like they are aiding their competition.

When you start finalizing your estimates, be sure to keep a log of how you came up with the number (a simple notebook or spreadsheet will do). If the data are particularly relevant or unique, you can include them in an appendix.

Operating Budget

Similar in format to the start-up budget above, the operating budget is a spending plan for all of the things you will need to run your cupcake business. The difference is that the analysis is for 3, 6, or 12 months, made up

44

of the ongoing expenses. The budget lists the type of expense and corresponding amount that will be paid on a monthly basis to keep the business operating.

Typical ongoing operating expenses include:

Advertising
Insurance
Utilities
Health Insurance
Loan Repayment (amount of interest and capital
   required to repay the loan each month). Indicate the
   terms of the loan.
Taxes
Payroll Tax Expenses
Medicare Tax Expense
Social Security Tax Expense
Rent
Payroll
Workman's Compensation Insurance
Supplies
Telephone
Water
GOGS (Cost of Goods Sold)
Maintenance/Repairs of Equipment
Accounting/Legal
Depreciation

Pro Forma Income Statement

A Pro Forma income statement is a look at **revenue** and **expense** projections for future periods. Based on your market research and a few assumptions, the pro forma statement will help you organize, evaluate, and quantify the results. The pro forma income statement will help you form an idea of what it will take to make a profit and be successful. This document is important in a business plan because it communicates the economic viability of your cupcake bakery to your financiers. The table provided below is for one year. Although some bankers and investors require one-, three-, or five-year estimates, a single year is usually sufficient in constructing a pro forma income statement. The pro forma income statement does not arrive at the true net income (or loss) for your bakery because variables such as depreciation, income taxes, interest, and utility hookups are not easily estimated.

The first item is the projected Revenue. You should have already calculated this in the Sales Forecast (Table 1). Likewise you will pull the **Unit Sales** and **COGS** from your sales forecast (Table 1), Your **Expenses** will be determined by your research and estimations from the **Operating Budget**. Chapters 10 and 11 will address in greater detail the expenses you will encounter and will assist you in compiling accurate estimations.

When everything is added up, the result is a one-year analysis. Your profit projections should be accompanied by a paragraph or two explaining how you estimated your income and expenses. Keep careful notes on your research and assumptions, so that you can explain them later if necessary, and also so that you can go back to your sources when it's time to revise your plan.

Table 3: Pro Forma Income Statement (Add the Date And Year)

Annual Gross Profit		
Projected sales		**$100,000**
Less Direct Costs		
Raw Ingredients	$10,000	
Sub-Contractors	$10,000	
Direct Labor	$25,000	
Total Direct Costs		**$45,000**
Gross Profit		**$55,000**
Gross Profit Margin		
Gross Profit	$55,000	
Sales	$100,000	
Gross Profit Margin		**55.0%**
Overheads		
Audit / Accounting Fees	$100	
Bus Dev. - Travel	$250	
Bus. Dev. - Entertainment	$500	
Bus. Dev. - Meals	$500	
Capital Acquisitions	n/a	
Charitable Contributions	$100	

Start a Cupcake Business Today

Commissions	$250	
Conferences and Seminars	$100	
Consulting Fees	$0	
Depreciation	$250	
Employee Benefits	$0	
Entertainment	$150	
Equipment Lease	$100	
Facilities - Insurance	$100	
Facilities - Phone	$500	
Facilities - Property Taxes	$0	
Facilities - Rent	$0	
Facilities - Security	$0	
Facilities - Utilities	$250	
Facility - Other	$0	
Financial Charges	$0	
Furniture	$150	
Insurance	$250	
Inventory Purchases	n/a	
IT Consulting	$0	
Legal Fees	$100	
Loan Capital	n/a	
Loan Interest	$0	
Miscellaneous	$500	
Office Supplies	$250	
Payroll - Operational staff	n/a	
Payroll - Administrative Staff	$0	
Payroll - Owner / Directors	$0	
Payroll - Sales / Marketing	$0	
Payroll Taxes	$0	
Postal / Shipping	$500	
PR / Advertising	$500	

Repairs and Maintenance	$250	
Research and Development	$0	
Storage	$0	
Subscriptions and Dues	$100	
Taxes and Licenses	$500	
Telecommunications	$100	
Vehicle Expenses	$250	
Overheads		**$6,600**
Break-even point (Annual)		
Overheads	$6,600	
Gross Profit Margin	55.0%	
Break-even point		**$12,000**
Break-even point (Monthly)		
Overheads	$6,600	
Gross Profit Margin	55.0%	
Break-even point		**$1,000**
Estimated Profit		
Projected Annual Sales	$100,000	
Break-Even Sales	$12,000	
	$88,000	
Gross Profit Margin	55.0%	

Estimated Profit		$48,40 0

*Note: the figures used in this table are not representative of a working cupcake business. Rather, they are simple numbers to illustrate the breakdown of data. A template is provided on our website for you to provide your actual numbers.

Break-Even Analysis

A break-even analysis predicts the sales volume (the quantity of cupcakes sold), at a given price, required to recover total costs. Simply stated, a break-even analysis helps you determine if you can make enough money each month to cover your expenses at the prices you set for your cupcakes. You need to bring your best estimations to this process and understand some basic concepts. A break-even analysis is included in most business plans because it shows at a very high level the initial goals the entrepreneur must set. While there are mathematical formulas used to calculate the break-even analysis, the easiest method is to use a web-based break-even calculator.

Web Resource: http://tinyurl.com/cupcakebreak
Use this online calculator to help determine your break-even point, the amount of revenue you need to generate to cover your monthly costs.

PLANNING FOR SUCCESS

To determine if your cupcake bakery will be viable, you must first estimate how much revenue you will bring in each month with a sales forecast. (See: Table 1.) While the estimates generated by your own research are a great starting point, ultimately, you should rely on a good local accountant with food service experience or someone who understands the restaurant or bakery business to confirm your numbers.

When calculating your break-even point, you need to know a few additional data variables. The first element is the **unit cost per item** (or cost of goods sold) that you sell. For a cupcake business, this is called **costing** your recipe, or adding up how much each recipe costs you to make (down to the penny).

The first step in recipe costing, is adding up the cost of the ingredients used. Since you may be purchasing items in bulk, you should calculate the price for a single unit of weight (grams or kilograms) for the entire bag, bottle, carton, etc. of each ingredient. In other words, if you buy a 50 pound bag of flour the first step is to convert it to kilograms, then calculate the cost of each kilogram.

The price of flour in bulk is $21.59 for a 50-pound or 22.7 kilogram bag. and thus the cost is $0.95 per kilograms. (21.59 ÷ 22.7) With that rate, convert your recipes to kilograms and determine how much of each ingredient is used to make a batch.

To save time converting your non-metric weights, use a specialized cooking conversion calculator:

Web Resource: http://tinyurl.com/cupcakecalc

Note, a good scale that measures in grams and/or kilograms will also save a great deal of time.

If you are not familiar with measuring your recipes by weight, you should learn this process. Measuring by weight has many advantages including:

Greater Accuracy: Weight is more accurate than volume, since it isn't affected by how well packed or sifted, finely or coarsely chopped, etc. the ingredient is.

Simplicity: It's quicker and simpler. By measuring directly into the mixing bowl, there are no measuring cups to level off, no messes from leveling off measuring cups, less need for sifting, and no dirty measuring cups to wash.

Commercial recipes: Recipes can specify any weight, without being restricted to the specific sizes of measuring cups available. There is no more need for oddball measures like "one cup minus two tablespoons" as is seen in some recipes.

Once you know the base unit price of a kilogram of flour, sugar, baking soda, etc., you convert your recipe into kilograms. For example, if your recipe calls for 31.5 oz of all-purpose flour, it will convert to 0.89 kg. The total cost of flour used in this recipe is $0.84

Ingredient	Price /kg	Cost/ingredient in recipe
All Purpose Flour	0.9511	0.8366125
White Sugar	1.5000	1.106625
Vegetable Oil	5.13	2.33
Cocoa Powder	6.6079	0.234
Vanilla Extract	32.6344	0.130537445
Baking Soda	1.6035	0.018958333
Buttermilk	8.8079	1.999403974
Eggs	4.1500	0.415
Salt	0.9362	0.011068945800

The recipe above makes 32 cupcakes. Dividing the total cost of all the ingredients by the number of cupcakes will provide you with the total cost per cupcake (about $0.22). When you add in labor, packaging, taxes and some measure of human error, the total cost ends up being about $0.69 per cupcake and about $0.20 for frosting.

Don't worry if this seems too difficult. On our website, we provide a handy tool for doing these calculations. (www.cupcake-business.com/resources). Once you know how much a single cupcake costs to make, you have a much greater appreciation for maximizing the efficiency of your operation, keeping a keen eye on your supplies and suppliers, and most importantly, setting your prices for profit.

This first calculation is known in accounting terms as the Costs of Goods Sold (or COGS). Once you have converted and costed out all of your recipes, you average them. Let's say the average cost for each recipe is $0.90 and you sell a cupcake for $3.00 on average (your average per-unit revenue).

You will make a profit, **before expenses**, of $2.10. How many cupcakes do you need to sell each month to pay your bills? This is known as your break-even point.

In order to figure your break-even point, you need your **estimated running costs**. This includes your payroll, rent, loan payment, utilities, etc. Let's assume you have $6,300 in expenses each month. Use the worksheet provided on our website to estimate your expenses. Do not include the cost to make the cupcake (COGS).

Using the break-even formula (**Break-even Point = Fixed Costs/(Unit Selling Price - Variable Costs)** or more simply a break-even calculator, your cupcake business would need $13,000 in revenue to meet all of the $6,300 in expenses. If you only sold cupcakes and no other products, you would have to sell 4,285 cupcakes per month or 165 cupcakes per day to break even.

If you estimate your daily process, such as when you start baking in the morning, how many batches you can make with the number of ovens you plan to have, the time required to make sales, and run the business, etc. you should be able to estimate the cupcake output of a single person. Your numbers should reflect realistic assumptions. If your operation requires higher output, that means additional staff and additional costs. One way to increase profits without increasing labor costs is to offer the right product mix – selling other products that are low labor, and high profit, such as beverages.

While figuring out a break even point is great for knowing the viability of a business, the reality is that for most people starting a business is far more than breaking even! It is making a good living. A second approach to forecasting is to set the starting point at the amount of profit you want to make to meet your lifestyle goals and pay off any debt.

For this approach you must determine, how much net profit you want the business to generate during the calendar year. How much will it cost to produce that profit? How much sales revenue is necessary to support both profit and costs?

Projected Cash Flow

In simple terms, to pay your bills, you have to have more cash coming in than going out. Sometimes, when business is strong, supplies are plentiful, and labor is "cheap," this is easy. More often than not however, it takes a watchful eye, fiscal restraint and careful cashflow management to make sure the cash going out is not in excess of the cash flowing in. Businesses fail because they cannot pay their bills. Every part of your business plan is important, but none of it means a thing if you run out of cash.

The point of preparing a projected cash flow is to plan how much you need before start-up, for preliminary expenses, operating expenses, and reserves. You should keep updating it and using it afterward. It will enable you to foresee shortages in time to do something about them— perhaps cut expenses, or perhaps negotiate a loan. But foremost, you shouldn't be taken by surprise.

There is no great trick to preparing it: The cash-flow projection is just a forward look at your checking account. For each item, determine when you actually expect to receive cash (for sales) or when you will actually have to write a check (for expense items).

You should track essential operating data, which are not necessarily part of cash flow but allow you to track items that have a heavy impact on cash flow, such as sales and inventory purchases. You should also track cash outlays that will be necessary prior to opening, in a pre-start-up column. You should have already researched those for your start-up expenses plan.

Your cash flow will reveal whether your working capital is adequate. Clearly, if your projected cash balance ever goes negative, you will need more start-up capital. This plan will also predict when and how much you will need to borrow.

Explain your major assumptions and address any of the following questions:

- If you provide cupcakes for a large wedding order in month one, when do you actually collect the cash?
- When you buy ingredients, do you pay in advance, upon delivery, or much later?
- How will this affect cash flow?
- Are some expenses payable in advance? When?
- Are there irregular expenses, such as quarterly tax payments, maintenance and repairs, or seasonal expenses such as additional staff during the holidays, which should be budgeted?

Loan payments, equipment purchases, and owner's draws usually do not show on profit and loss statements but since they do take cash out and therefore are important to a cash flow projection. And of course, depreciation does not appear in the cash flow at all because you never write a check for it.

		Month x	
		Budget	Actual
Revenue			
Receipts			
Cash Sales			
Loans received			
Grants received			
Other income			
Capital injected			
Asset Disposal			
Total Receipts		$0.00	$0.00
Payments			
Material Purchases - Cash			
Material Purchases - Creditors			
Sub-Contractors			
Audit / Accounting Fees			
Bus Dev. - Travel			
Bus. Dev. - Entertainment			
Bus. Dev. - Meals			
Capital Acquisitions			
Charitable Contributions			
Commissions			
Conferences & Seminars			
Consulting Fees			
Depreciation		n/a	n/a
Employee Benefits			
Entertainment			
Equipment Lease			
Facilities - Insurance			
Facilities - Phone			
Facilities - Property Taxes			
Facilities - Rent			
Facilities - Security			

	Facilities - Utilities		
	Facility - Other		
	Financial Charges		
	Furniture		
	Insurance		
	IT Consulting		
	Legal Fees		
	Loan Capital		
	Loan Interest		
	Miscellaneous		
	Office Supplies		
	Payroll - Operational staff		
	Payroll - Administrative Staff		
	Payroll - Owner / Directors		
	Payroll - Sales / Marketing		
	Payroll Taxes		
	Postal / Shipping		
	PR / Advertising		
	Repairs & Maintenance		
	Research and Development		
	Storage		
	Subscriptions & Dues		
	Taxes & Licenses		
	Telecommunications		
	Vehicle Expenses		
Total Payments		$0.00	$0.00
Net Cash Flow		$0.00	$0.00
Opening Cash Balance		$0.00	$0.00
	Receipts	$0.00	$0.00
	Payments	$0.00	$0.00
Closing Cash Balance		$0.00	$0.00

Opening Day Balance Sheet

A balance sheet is one of the fundamental financial reports that any business needs to understand and keep track of the value of the business. If for example you are seeking a loan, the bank will use a balance sheet to assess your net worth and evaluate your credit-worthiness. In the most basic terms, a balance sheet is a list of everything of value -- your checking and savings account, mutual funds, house, cars, 401k-- that you own and a list of everything you owe to creditors --mortgage, car payments, and other loans. You subtract everything you owe by all the stuff you have and come up with your net worth. Remember, if you are seeking financing from a bank, they are looking at your personal finances. If this is a start up business, there is probably no company assets or liabilities. If you are purchasing an existing cupcake bakery, then a balance sheet would be provided by the sellers, showing you what items of value are held by the company (assets), and what its debts are (liabilities). Just as with a personal balance sheet, when liabilities are subtracted from assets, the remainder is the owners' equity.

Use the spreadsheets provided in our website resources section as a guide to calculate what your opening day balance sheet. When adding to your business plan, detail how you calculated the account balances. Optional: Some people want to add a projected balance sheet showing the estimated financial position of the business at the end of the first year. This is especially useful when selling your proposal to investors.

Assets	
Current Assets	
Cash	$2,000
Other Current Assets	
401 K	
Stocks	
Total Current Assets	$10,000
	$5,000
Long-term Assets	$300
Equity in Home (123 Main Street, Oxford OH, 45056)	$150
2004 Honda Accord EX	$9,092
Subtotal Long-term Assets	$500
Total Assets	$150
	$100
Liabilities and Capital	$1,000
	0
Current Liabilities	
Accounts Payable	$650
Auto Loan Payments	$295
Mortgage	$2,200
Subtotal Current Liabilities	$3,145
Long-term Liabilities	
Mortgage	289,000
Student Loan	37,000
Auto Loan	4,500
Subtotal Long-term Liabilities	
Total Liabilities	
Net Worth	

BUSINESS PLAN APPENDICES

Include details and studies used in your business plan, for example:

- Advertising materials
- Blueprints and plans of your shop
- Maps and photos of location
- Magazine or web articles
- Detailed lists of equipment owned or to be purchased
- Copies of leases and contracts
- Letters of support from future customers
- Any other materials needed to support the assumptions in this plan
- Market research studies
- List of assets available as collateral for a loan

THE FINANCIAL PLAN

Most small business owners end up leveraging their personal assets (and those of friends and family members) to launch their business. This is because in many cases, commercial lenders balk at providing start up capital for an unproven business that has no revenues to prove the loan will be repaid on time.

Financing in recent years has been made more difficult stemming from new due diligence requirements coming out of the 2008-2009 economic recession, during which time credit and cash flow all but dried up.

It's not impossible to obtain financing to start your business, but in order to obtain it, you need to be very clear about your business plan and be willing to commit your own resources to demonstrate your personal investment in the business.

When it comes to financing your cupcake business, there are a few options available to you. One, you can use your own credit cards and personal finances to open the business. Two, you can seek commercial financing from a bank or using an SBA-backed loan. Three, you can seek angel investments to fund your business. Each choice has its advantages and disadvantages.

Using Your Own Money

The biggest hurdle here is, of course, if you don't have your own money to use. If you don't have credit cards with open credit balances and you don't have $100,000 in equity you can pull out of your house; if you don't have stocks, bonds, retirement, or savings accounts you can draw from...you are like most people who want to start a business from the ground up.

The first advantage of using your personal finances to open your business is that you remain completely in control creatively. You don't have to do anything to meet commercial lender requirements; you don't have to let an investment company control an interest in your business. If you can afford it, and afford to lose it, without affecting your quality of life, personally financing your venture (or personally financing it with the help of family or friends) might be the best option for you.

The second advantage of self-financing, at least, in part, is that if you do want/need additional funding, it shows outside investors that you believe in your business enough to invest your own money. This is crudely known as "skin in the game," a term coined by Warren Buffet meaning putting one's own money on the line just like outside investors.

Even if you do have the personal assets available that you can leverage, you need to be careful. Businesses do fail, and if you've tied up your life savings in the business, you will lose a lot more than a great idea.

The disadvantage to using your personal finances to launch the business is that if you've tied up all of your assets, run up the credit balances on your credit cards, and pulled the equity out of your house, you have nothing left to make you credit-worthy when you do need to seek commercial lending for a capital infusion or to grow the business. And, if for some reason it takes longer to start generating revenue than you expected, you could very well end up with your personal credit being tarnished in the process. That is why the amount of "skin in the game" is a balancing act –putting enough of your own money to project the confidence you have in your cupcake business, but not too much that you've ruined your credit.

According to the SBA, 80% of all small businesses are funded all or in part with personal funds. If you do plan to use your own money to start your cupcake business, you need to plan on having access to $50,000-$250,000 depending on the size of the business, its location, and the associated costs. If you don't have all the money you need, it may be possible to work something out with friends and family to assist with the rest.

Using Your 401(k)

In many cases, 401(k) savings can be used for small business start-up costs without being penalized for early withdraw or higher tax rates.

Using your retirement to finance your business is a risk only you and your financial advisor can make, understanding that many businesses fail within the first year. However, many businesses fail because of a lack of capital, so if you have a good business plan and just need the money to make it happen, it might be a worthy risk.

Since other lending options can come with as much risk as using 401(k) savings, it's often a very attractive choice. Not only do you avoid having to qualify for commercial lending or commit your personal assets to guarantee the loan, but you also avoid having to give up control to an investor.

There are two different ways you can use your 401(k) savings to start your business. In one method, the process is similar to taking a loan against your 401(k) but the maximum cash you can take is $50,000 or 50% of the balance of your 401(k) and if you default on the loan repayment, you'll be nailed with the extra taxes (unless you are over the age of 59½).

The other method may require the assistance of a CPA or tax attorney who is familiar with the ROBS loan (Rollovers as Business Start-Ups). In this method, a firm will help you create a 401(k) plan for your new business using the funds from your old 401(k). The 401(k) then purchases stock in the company, furnishing you with the start-up capital you need.

Commercial Lenders
It is a harsh reality for many aspiring business owners that commercial lenders are not in the start-up business investment industry. They lend money when they can guarantee to the best of their ability, that the money will be repaid, with interest. Often, they will only loan to businesses that have been in business for at least three years. Remember, a commercial bank's goal is to achieve the highest possible rates of return while mitigating risk.

If you are not an established business with provable revenue, you may find it difficult to obtain commercial lending. However, commercial lenders who participate with the Small Business Administration may be more willing to help with your business if you meet certain criteria. In most cases, though, if the business is not already up and running, you may have to guarantee the loan personally, meaning if the business goes under, you will still be responsible for the loan payments.

Your business plan will be very important when applying for a loan. In addition to the documents from Chapter 3 that you've created, be sure to indicate in an appendix the amount of loan you are seeking, how the funds will be used and the requested repayment terms (number of years to repay), collateral offered (home, automobile, etc.), and a list of all existing liens against collateral (e.g. existing loans)

For most businesses, the most common source of third-party financing is through the Small Business Administration (SBA). The SBA has two main programs available for business loans, the 7A and the 504. The SBA does not fund loans but provides government guarantees to a portion of each loan made by private banks participating in the program.

To have the best possible shot at obtaining a commercial loan, having a solid business plan is absolutely essential. Your business plan should be well researched and contain an in-depth SWOT analysis. SWOT stands for strengths, weaknesses, opportunities, and threats. Strengths and weaknesses are internal factors. Opportunities and threats are external factors. The advantage of obtaining bank funding is the rapid funding of the loan and the ability to get up and running relatively quickly.

During the economic crisis of 2009, there was a 60% drop in SBA lending, but even when lending is not as restricted, typically owners must be "credit qualified" — their personal credit rating must be high — in order to qualify. The U.S. government has been crucial in the fight to secure additional credit opportunities for small businesses, encouraging the Small Business Administration to provide more government-backed loans.

There are two programs available from the SBA that often help small businesses with their financial needs, particularly if you are buying an existing bakery or cupcake shop with a history of profitability.

7A Loan Program

This loan program is the most flexible offering from the SBA and is designed to help existing small businesses obtain the financing they need, particularly if they are not eligible for other loans. Because the loans are designed to be flexible, they can be used in a variety of different industries for a number of purposes, including purchase. Loan terms are 10 years for capital and up to 25 years for assets.

Both commercial banks and non-bank lenders can participate in the 7A lending program, so the availability of the loans is increased. Even though the SBA guarantees a percentage of the loan, if a lender determines that the loan carries too much risk, the SBA cannot force them to give the loan. There are certain eligibility factors that must be met, but it is an excellent source of third-party financing in most cases.

504 Loan Program

The SBA 504 Loan program has much more specific criteria, including job creation requirements. The loans from this program are often targeted toward revitalization areas and are only available to for-profit businesses. As well, these loans must be used for fix-asset projects.

In all cases where financing is required, it is important for you as the seller to know up front what kind of arrangements you are willing to make. Often, if you are under pressure to sell, you may need to consider arrangements other than straight third-party financing, like allowing a portion of the purchase to be paid through the business revenues, or by partnering with the buyer for a specified length of time.

Depending on your financial situation, you may even be in a position to carry a portion of the loan as long as the buyer is able to secure a down payment of a sufficient amount.

Investors

Investors have a different perspective than commercial lenders. Investors typically provide funds needed in the short term as they are looking for quick turn-around and they expect to share in the rewards.

In your business plan indicate how your cupcake business would use any funds provided by investors; estimated return on investment; an exit strategy for investors (the method for recouping their investment); percent of ownership that you will give up to investors; milestones or conditions that you will accept; financial reporting to be provided; involvement of investors on the board or in management

Peer to Peer Lending

The advent of peer to peer lending has created new sources of funding for entrepreneurs. Sites like Prosper.com and Lending Club work in the same way as an eBay auction. To get started, it is free to set up an account. Be sure to read their guidelines and the types of loans their lenders fund. Prosper does not officially fund business loans but they do fund entrepreneurs who want to start a small business. Once you have familiarized yourself with the system and browsed other successful listings, post the amount of the loan you need and the maximum interest rate you will pay on their online auction site. You want to convey with confidence and hard numbers, your proposal. You must have a good personal credit score to qualify for a loan, usually 640 or more.

Your loan request will go into a 7-day auction. Lenders bid on your loan and, as they do, your interest rate may go down. If you change your mind and decide you don't want/need the loan, you can stop the auction.

The interest rate and monthly payments are fixed and there is a one-time closing fee. When paying back the loan, there is no charge for prepayment. The loan is unsecured, which means you do not have to put up any collateral to guarantee the loan. All of their loans are 3-year fully amortized loans funded through WebBank. To obtain a fair interest rate, however, you still need to have a strong personal credit rating. Rates can be as low as 7.5% for those with good credit, and can even be bid lower by lenders. The interest rate can be worse than credit card rates for those whose credit is rated a D or D-.

When you apply for a loan on Prosper, you provide profile information that authorizes Prosper to rate your credit based on an electronic credit check. There is no way to adjust the rating they give you, but you are allowed to explain your credit situation in your narrative.

Another peer to peer lender to check out is Lending Club. The terms may vary slightly but the principle is basically the same. Peer to peer lending organizations connect willing lenders and investors with borrowers who have the opportunity to make a more direct appeal to their potential investors.

Angel Investors
A commonly overlooked source of funding is that of angel investors. These investors, unlike commercial banks, are willing to take more extraordinary risk and will often provide funding for start-ups in exchange for some interest in the business. The advantage of this kind of funding is that no immediate payback, if any, is required. The disadvantage is, of course, someone else having any kind of say in the way you run your cupcake shop. However, these financial deals can often be structured in such a way as to meet everyone's approval.

How do you find an angel investor?

Friends and Family
Interest rates are dismal for money sitting in savings accounts right now, making it an ideal opportunity for friends and family to take some of their savings and put it into your business for a better return. The advantage: you have a built-in level of trust. The disadvantage: if something goes wrong, you may live to regret it, especially when your uncle complains at every family reunion about how you took his money.

If you take a loan from a family member, the most important way you can protect your business and your relationship with your family is to treat your family angel like a business partner.

Draw up a detailed contract that specifies how and when your lender will be repaid, how much interest will be paid, and what, if any, control the family member gains in the bakery. It is crucial to have an attorney draw up your agreement. Don't think that because it's your parents or your cousin that money won't make it difficult to work out problems. Specify everything in writing.

Woo Your Angels

When you are trying to attract strangers to invest in your cupcake shop, they are going to need more concrete reasons to invest. This is easier for technology companies, who often can present a prototype of the company so that the investor can see how the company would work. With a bakery, you need to present a solid business plan with revenue projections. You can enhance your appeal by providing references or letters from potential customers stating that they would purchase your products or contract with you for catering services, parties or weddings at the prices you have established.

Find Angels Online

Keep in mind that many angel investors want to make a difference. Do your homework and find angels who like to develop communities or help women become business owners. The more you understand about how to appeal to your angel, the more likely it will be that you will be able to obtain some support in financing your dream.

Give your angel a role

Inviting a potential angel to work with your business in the capacity of an advisor can help elevate his or her interest in your success. Start-up companies can be an exciting challenge...it's where the dreams are. Your angel may be craving an opportunity to share hard-earned experience and knowledge with you, and once invested emotionally in your success, your angel will often be more willing to invest financially as well.

When you do find an angel investor, you need to have some flexibility about the terms of the deal they will make with you. The advantage of an angel investor is that you get the cash you need without the pressure of repayment before you can make a profit. That advantage however, is often accompanied by the investor wanting some creative control or decision-making power. You need to decide what is important and what isn't before negotiating your deal.

Get Creative with Funding

Most small business start-ups have to use a variety of funding options to obtain the capital they need. One way to give people an incentive to invest is to sell "stock" in your company that provides a direct and ongoing benefit to the small community investor. This idea of selling community shares in your company is one way to raise money for your bakery's start-up costs. For example, a $500 investment could entitle the shareholder to one free cupcake a week or a dozen cupcakes each year plus a 10% discount for life

DEVELOPING YOUR BRAND

To be visible in the twenty-first century, even if you are a local shop with no plans to expand beyond your town or neighborhood, your brand identity is critical to your success. You don't have to be a major brand name to be profitable, but you do want cohesive representation of what your business is. Your brand identity should emanate from your physical location, through your products and remain consistent through your logo, your website, and all of your marketing materials.

Take a moment now to write down a draft of your mission statement. A mission statement is a concise paragraph describing what your company does and for whom. It is the essence of your brand. Here is an example from California's SugarBowl Bakery:

> Sugar Bowl Bakery's mission is to produce and market the highest quality baked goods and continue to develop a brand name that inspires trust and quality. We will achieve this by hiring the best people, providing quality customer

71

care and service and giving back to our community.

A mission statement needs to be simple and brief enough that anyone reading it quickly understands your company's most basic goals – your mission. Over time, as you work on setting up your business, you may want to return to your mission statement and revise or fine-tune it.

In addition to writing your mission statement, you should also take the time to write your WHY statement. This is a personal statement, not for public eyes. Whenever starting something big, time-consuming, or otherwise important, it helps to understand your WHY.

That is, *why* are you doing this? Take a moment now to write down and preserve your reasons for starting a cupcake bakery, cupcake truck, wholesale vendor or whatever your dream. Knowing your why is an often neglected first step in starting a business; yet as you get going, and challenges inevitably arise, you can always return to the foundation of your business, your why. Do this now while you are thinking of it. It needn't be a lengthy document or polished for anyone else's reading. Just write freely what comes to you.

Logo

One of the most critical graphic design elements of your branding strategy is your logo. Your logo is your visual identity in the same way as your business name. In fact, if your design is successful, people are just as likely to associate you with your logo as they are your name. Consider how many food companies are recognized around the globe by their signature logos. For example: Coca-Cola's red and white script and unique bottle, McDonald's golden arches, Quaker Oats' smiling quaker. These symbols have grown in our consciousness and have enabled their associated brands to grow in consumer loyalty and profit. If you take the time to think about the significance of logos, no matter what the brand, you can understand how they are created to inspire trust, recognition and admiration.

Your logo should be unique enough to make people think of your business every time they see it, but not so confusing or complicated that your customers don't know what it is. For a specialty shop, something that is associated with the type of product you sell or induces your customers to think of your name is important. For example, if you are primarily a cupcake business that caters to brides, your logo should be more evocative of something elegant. If you plan to have a high energy, playful kind of experience you might incorporate colorful, whimsical elements in the design.

A logo is so important that you may want to outsource this effort to a professional designer. The internet has made it much easier and cost effective to find suitable designers who can help you create this kind of branding collateral. If you are familiar with local design resources, it is nice to be able to meet with someone in person; however, if you've never hired a graphic artist, the internet enables you to draw from a huge pool of talent and thus more people are competing for your graphic design business. The result is higher quality work, more choices and lower costs. Here are a few websites you should consider for your design needs:

- LogoFactory http://www.thelogofactory.com/
- LogoBee [http://www.logobee.com]
- LogoLoft [http://www.logoloft.com]

Of course, even when you are hiring someone to do design work, you should educate yourself about what constitutes an effective logo and remain active in the process. Do not hesitate to ask questions, provide criticism, and get the results you want. If there is something your designer provides that you do not understand or with which you disagree, make them explain their thinking. This is a give and take relationship, and one for which you are paying.

Here are a few simple guidelines to follow when choosing (or designing) your logo.

1. A logo must be able to be described accurately in a single sentence or phrase. If your logo can't be translated into words with ease, it won't be effective as a marketing tool. Your customers should be able to understand and share the concept of your logo: "A big pink box," "A child holding a cupcake"
2. A logo must be memorable: This is subjective, but if your first impression says, "this is too generic" then, ask for alternatives. Keep in mind, memorable does not necessarily mean complex. In fact, a simple logo can be easier to reproduce and more importantly, easier to remember. Examples: Apple, Nike.
3. A logo must be effective without color. You are potentially going to be putting your logo on cards, boxes, cups, napkins, aprons, on doors and windows –everywhere. Your logo (or a version of it) should be just as effective coming from a stamp as it is from a four-color press.
4. A logo must be scalable: Again, because your logo will be used many places, it needs to be just as recognizable when it is an inch high as when it is 20 feet high.

When evaluating designs keep in mind that the logo:
*   Looks good on print materials (business card, letterhead, invoices) as well as your website
*   Could be made into a sign
*   Should be delivered in **Vector format** as well as **layered .psd** (Photoshop document) and **.jpg**
*   Is easy to distinguish from your competitors

Your logo will be used in all of your marketing materials so it needs to portray the essence of your business. Are you a traditional "mom-and-pop" shop, or more chic and upscale. Are you appealing primarily to a wedding clientele? Trying to brand a cupcake shop that also sells wedding cakes? Then a logo that incorporates both product lines could work. Understanding your theme is important.

Keep language and text separate from your logo. A textual treatment of your company name, e.g. "Sublime Cupcakes" is a common part of many logos. It's best to keep the visual and text elements separate (as opposed to overlapping, intertwining, etc). This way, you'll be able to use either the text or icon independently. Likewise, your tagline -- the phrase or few words that describe your cupcakes – should also be distinct elements. Your tagline or business name can be featured with your logo but if they are required elements they will require a small font that will become illegible at smaller sizes.

Text can also create a lot of visual clutter in many applications. There are appropriate places to use your tag line like your website and business cards.

Once you have created a logo, it should be placed on all materials: labels, order forms, signs, tags, business cards, brochures, stickers, etc. Your logo is key to product recognition. Some people respond to words while many others respond to images. Even if a customer can't remember the name, they'll remember the logo.

Cost saving idea: Create a black and white logo that can be printed in a variety of colors, made into a rubber stamp, printed on a black and white printer, etc. Sometimes, the simplest tools are the best. If, for example you provide paper bags for customers on the go, don't spend money on printing bags. Use your simple logo on boxes, invoices, flyers, letterhead or even business cards. Reserve the full logo for your door, website, press kit and sign.

Signage

Purchasing signage for your new business is expensive, but it is not a cost you should put off too long. Think about the businesses that you visit, both at home and when traveling. Isn't signage one of the most obvious ways we distinguish one place from another? An example of great signage execution is the Austin, Texas cupcake shop, Hey Cupcake! On each of their locations there is a huge cupcake with pink frosting and sprinkles. While the investment is significant, imagine the benefit of the instant recognition. This shop is so closely tied to its signage, that it sued another cupcake business for violating its trademark and using the big pink cupcake as its signage.

Being visible in your community is one of the most critical factors for the success of a bakery business. A good location combined with visible, well-designed signage can help drive traffic into your business, eliminating some of the need for costly marketing campaigns.

Before you invest in any signage, check the code regulations of your area. What type of sign has your city council, county planners or historic preservation commissioners deemed acceptable? Usually, your landlord can provide you with the necessary guidelines and local zoning ordinances which regulate the type, size, the height, the configuration, the color, the aesthetics, etc. of signage. For example, if you have neon (or a huge pink cupcake) in mind, and the local historic commission only permits, low profile placards, you want to know before investing in something that will end up in your garage rather than the front of your bakery.

Once you know the rules, you can approach a vendor. Chances are, if they are local, they are familiar with the UBC and local zoning requirements of your area. As long as you purchase or lease your sign from a reputable company, you should have no problems. Make sure that your contract with the sign company includes a clause that they are responsible that your sign meets requirements. Moreover, make sure the clause makes the company liable should any adjustment in your sign be necessary due to zoning regulations or other city or county codes. The company should also obtain the necessary construction and installation permits.

A well-conceived sign can be an excellent marketing tool. It should not only be reflective of the image you wish to project, but communicate important information about your cupcake business. Is there a vibe to your shop that you want to project - upscale, hip, gourmet, etc.? Put it on the sign. Signs communicate important information to potential customers. The sign should say something to draw in the customers in your immediate area.

Signage should be an important part of the promotional strategy in your business plan and should be included in your loan package.

There are other ways in which a sign compliments your business: it reinforces the other outreach tools such as your logo. Consumers who find you online, for example, will have greater ease finding your bakery location if the logo is used on your sign. In fact, your logo design and your sign should be similar if not exact. You are creating a brand and an integrated marketing plan. Your customers will remember your logo, colors and fonts, so choose them carefully.

A sign that is clearly visible from the road gives motorists ample time to stop and park, so be sure to use a typeface that is legible from a distance. Cursive or intricate fonts can be hard to read in any presentation.

A sign is a visual cue that customers can remember encouraging repeat business. A visible sign that is easy to understand can make the difference between success and failure. Many businesses attribute a large percentage of their business to their signs.

Once you have invested in a sign, it is to your advantage to keep it in good repair. If you lease through a reputable sign company, the maintenance of the sign can be made part of the contract. A dilapidated sign does not send the right message for a successful business. So, factor in maintenance to your costs if you will buy instead of lease. In addition to your location (discussed in detail in Chapter 7), signage can make the difference between success and failure.

Internet Marketing

According to Lehman Hailey, visibility expert and author of *The DNA of Internet Marketing*, brick and mortar businesses cannot survive well in the twenty-first century without broadening their reach through Internet marketing and the development of a clean, easy-to-navigate, well-organized website.

When you own an online shop, you naturally focus on the Internet for reaching customers and advertising your product or service, but according to Hailey, around 80% of consumers who are looking for a brick and mortar business in their own community start with an Internet search. If your name doesn't come up in that search, you are losing customers.

Website

Your website is as important as the physical signage on your building, according to Hailey. Your website is all about branding your business, making you recognizable, and telling your story. The two most common ways to establish a web presence are building a site from scratch using HTML, php, flash, etc. or using a content management system that enables you to plug your information into pre-defined content areas.

The first method requires that you have the skills to build a site or you can hire someone, while the second method, incorporates free tools such as Wordpress or Weebly and a good theme. The free or inexpensive route may serve as a temporary solution until you are ready to invest in a custom site.

The first step is to buy a domain (Hailey recommends buying the domain name as soon as possible, prior even to opening the business). Your domain name (which can cost as little as $10 per year) is ideally the same as your business name. Unfortunately, many of the best domain names are taken. Sometime, investors purchase common names in hopes to sell them to authentic businesses with the same name, and for significant profit.

According to Hailey, WordPress sites are great for branding and elegant, business-oriented themes are available to give your site a unique look. The page should be cleanly designed and provide information about your cupcake business and what kinds of products and services you offer. Do you specialize in wedding cupcakes or deliverable cupcake bouquets? Make sure your website reflects that.

Your presence on the web is your public face. It tells prospective customers who you are, where you're located, what you sell, and how much your goods might cost. Most importantly, it enables the customer to see pictures of your products, making you an irresistible temptation.

While many business owners try to write the copy for their website, it is always best to hire a professional copywriter to assist you in developing the language for your website. Most freelance writers are available at reasonable costs but can enhance both the quality of the writing and the search engine results that drive the name of your business to the top of the list.

Think of your website as part advertisement and part information. Your goal should be to:

- Explain what kinds of products and services you offer and convey a message of why the customer will benefit from choosing you.
- Create a website that is easy to navigate, with tabs or links to additional pages that are clearly marked.
- Include relevant contact information.
- Connect to your blog, online articles, and other relevant information on the web that establish you as an

industry insider.

Your website does not work just as a marketing tool with your customers. It also establishes your credibility within your industry, with your vendors, and for networking purposes. A website is flexible enough that it can be used in a number of ways. You may wish to work with the media, go to trade shows, contact buyers directly and use it to impress financial backers.

Online Directories

Even more important than being listed in your local yellow pages (although you should definitely do that too) is to make sure your business is listed in the local directory of Yahoo, Google, and other search engines. Once you've invested the time and expense in creating a great website for your business, you want to make sure it gets traffic.

These directories are a great way to increase your exposure and often allow customers to add comments and ratings, which you can encourage, your satisfied customers to do in order to help grow your reputation.

Getting your cupcake business listed on the local search engines sites will not only get more traffic to your website, but more importantly, more calls on the phone and more new customers in the door.

Local search listings include not only your basic contact information, but also a map of your business location. These listings are often given a very prominent position in the search engine results and they are free!

CitySearch.com /AOL Local / InfoUSA
(Both Citysearch.com and AOL Local use listing information from InfoUSA.com.)
- Step 1 – Go to InfoUSA.com
- Step 2 – Click 'Add Business Record'.
- Step 3 – Click 'Submit'.

Google Local

- **Step 1** – Go to Google Local to create a Google Account. You will need this to create your Google Maps listing. If you already have a Google Account, you can login here as well.
- **Step 2** – Enter your information, and Google will send you a confirmation email.
- **Step 3** – Click the confirmation link in the email to login to the Google Local Business Center.
- **Step 4** – Click 'Add New Business'.
- **Step 5** – Follow the steps and fill in your address, phone number, website, etc. You will also be given a chance to choose a category for your business, as well as enter your store hours, payment methods accepted, parking information and a wealth of other information about your cupcake bakery.
- **Step 6** – Once you have all of your information proofed and spell checked, click 'Submit'.
- **Step 7** – Google will then either need you to confirm your submission by calling a 1-800 number (faster) OR having a postcard sent to your physical address (slower). Your listing will not go live until you confirm it by one of these methods.
- **Step 8** – Once you have confirmed your submission, it will take 4-6 weeks to appear in the Google Maps listings, so be patient.

Yahoo Local

- **Step 1** – Go to Yahoo Local to create a Yahoo Account. You will need this to create your Yahoo Local listing. If you already have a Yahoo Account, you can login here as well.
- **Step 2** – Enter your information, and Yahoo will send you a confirmation email.
- **Step 3** – Click the confirmation link in the email

to login to the Yahoo Local Listings Center.

- **Step 4** – Follow the steps and fill in your address, phone number, website, etc. You will also be given a chance to choose a category for your business, as well as enter your store hours, payment methods accepted, parking information, etc.
- **Step 5** – Once you have all of your information proofed and spell checked, click 'Submit'.
- **Step 6** – Yahoo Local Listings show up in search results very quickly – typically within 5-10 business days.

Cityguides (MSN) / YellowPages.com

(MSN's City Guides uses listing information from YellowPages.com)

- **Step 1** – Go to YellowPages.com.
- **Step 2** – Enter your business phone number to see if your bakery is already included in the directory. If it is already included, you will have a chance to update your listing.
- **Step 3** – If you are not already listed, enter your information on the following screens.
- **Step 4** – Click 'Submit'.

Superpages.com

- **Step 1** – Go to Superpages.com.
- **Step 2** – Enter your business information.
- **Step 3** – Select a business category (bakery) that will help customers find your listing.
- **Step 4** – Review your listing and profile.
- **Step 5** – Enter account information.
- **Step 6** – Click 'Submit'.

Blog

Regardless of what service you choose to host your website, adding a blog is another great way to communicate with customers and establish yourself as a reliable expert in your industry. Research increasingly points to social networks and blogs as primary sources for consumers to find information about brands and businesses.

You don't have to wait until you're in business to start reaching out to your community. Blogging is used by many successful cupcake business owners to attract an audience before they've even opened. One popular example, started in 2007, is Retro Baker's *Building a Bakery* blog. The owners document their entire process of starting a bakery in Las Vegas, Nevada.

It is a fascinating and educational read for anyone starting a food business. **http://tinyurl.com/retroarchive.**

Once you are established, blogging will increase the number of visitors to your website. Many small businesses struggle with the lack of search engine results for their website. They spend time and money in developing an internet presence yet, Google and Yahoo do not rank their sites very highly for the search terms that will bring potential new customers. According to a 2010 HubSpot survey, companies that blog have far better marketing results. Specifically, the average company that blogs has:

- 55% more visitors
- 97% more inbound links
- 434% more indexed pages

What this means is blogging will increase the likelihood that when people in your community look online for cupcakes, your business comes up first in the search. The major search engines are looking for relevant content. When you take the time to write about your latest creations, special ingredients you're incorporating, beautiful photographs of your product or simply future developments with your cupcake bakery, the search engine "spiders" are identifying your site as an authority on a particular subject. The main thing is that there is activity on your site and that the text is related to the search terms your prospective customers are seeking. Our resource guide in the appendix lists several easy-to-use, often free website tools that can help you build a professional website.

If you feel like website optimization is too difficult for you, you can work with a writer or SEO (search engine optimization) expert. The objective is to develop a set of keywords or phrases that describe your business and can be incorporated into your blog articles to help drive the right kind of traffic to your website. The most obvious keywords you should target are "cupcakes" + your community. (e.g. wedding cupcakes Atlanta or best cupcakes Syracuse)

Think about how the customer searches for a product and write down those words (keywords). Incorporate these keywords into your website text. You can also outsource the design of your website and blog if you are not technically proficient. In fact, Hailey recommends outsourcing these types of services so that you can stay focused on running your bakery. However, if you can do this work yourself, there are great resources available for free online. A basic blogging primer can be found here: **http://tinyurl.com/bakeryblog**

Press Releases

Publishing press releases about your business is another way to take advantage of both online and offline marketing. Online, your press release can be submitted to free and paid submission services and include links back to your website, which improves your page's search engine ranking. Prweb.com is one of the best-known press release distribution services, though it is a paid service. Free examples include:

- prleap.com
- prlog.org
- prcompass.com

Your goal is to be the first item on the list when someone is looking for a cupcake bakery in your area. You can publish press releases regularly, focusing on an event, holiday, or happening in your business. Most online press release submission sites also allow photos, which can allow you to show off your products.

Offline press releases can be submitted to your local newspaper, announcing the opening of your business, specials you are offering, or events in which your business is involved. You can include coupons or special offers in your locally printed press releases as well.

Some entrepreneurs fail to take advantage of the potential of a press release, assuming they are not relevant in the age of the internet. However, local newspapers still rely on press releases and many online resources pull information from press release aggregators or hubs as a way to research new content. While email marketing, social networking, Twitter and other web-based opportunities should be incorporated into your overall marketing approach, traditional media such as newspaper and television should not be overlooked. Thus, a well-written press release is an integral part of your overall press kit. If you need additional help, consider Janet Meiners Thaeler's book: *I Need a Killer Press Release--Now What???: A Guide to Online PR* **http://tinyurl.com/bakerypr**

Social Media Marketing

By now, you should be well aware of the huge potential impact the internet can have on launching your small business. Your customers use the web more than any other medium to research the products and services they are considering. This is true both for big brands such as Martha Stewart and local businesses such as cupcake shops. For many small businesses, social media is one of the most cost effective ways to reach a new audience.

Facebook

Developing a Facebook (www.Facebook.com) page for your business is an important step that is technically simple, but requires some finesse to be effective. Facebook pages are often a business' second home on the Web. Unless you are well versed in social media marketing, it is important to keep a few guidelines in mind when using Facebook (or any social network) in your marketing plan. First of all, an online social network is surprisingly similar to offline networking. Just because you are behind a keyboard rather than face-to-face, you should not disregard established conventions. Many businesses want to make an impact quickly and mistake social networking as an opportunity to start advertising to a large audience.

Social marketing requires an investment in time. Your network, many of whom may be customers, are looking for value from any social networking relationship. They are experienced to know if someone in their network simply wants to spam them with advertising rather than creating real value. For it to be worthwhile for anyone other than friends and family to join your network, you need to have two-way conversations and provide value.

If you are unfamiliar with social networking and marketing, here are some simple ways to use Facebook effectively:

1.   Put all of your contact information on your page: While your fan/business page is a great start, customers want to learn more about you. Make it easy for them to get to know you and your busi-

ness. Include your URL so people can find your website. Write in a simple, direct way. Your business description should be written not only for those who already know you, but also potential customers. If you are open for business, make it obvious where you are located, your hours of operation and what kind of cupcakes and any other products and services you offer.

2.   Post same-day news about special products, flavors, discounts, coupons, etc. Once you've made the effort to attract a fan base, you need to keep them engaged with frequent posts; otherwise, they will lose interest in your business. Are you trying a new recipe? Do you have a limited supply of a special product? Tell your fans.

3.   Post photographs. Nothing grabs our attention and whets our appetite like stunning images of foods we love. Remember, Facebook is a means to getting people in your shop. Seeing your cupcakes is an effective way to draw an audience to your physical location.

4.   Write about a variety of topics – not just your products. Intersperse product-related posts with topics that share your bakery's personality. For example, you can write about behind-the-scenes details such as how you got started, new business developments in your neighborhood, special ingredients you're trying. People love to hear about the "romantic" aspects of operating a cupcake business. Your posts on Facebook can sell not just individual products, but your shop as a destination. What do you love about owning a cupcake business? Make your post something readers/fans look forward to seeing. Example: **http://tinyurl.com/floursunbakery**

5.   Ask your customers for advice. Today's consumers love to be invited into the process. Look for opportunities where your customers can provide

feedback. For example, cupcake bakeries often seek advice about new flavors. In an environment with such creativity and range of tastes, a bakery can reinforce the loyalty of their clients by making them feel invested and listened to.

6.   Become connected with fans of other local businesses and other bakeries. Remember, using Facebook effectively means viewing it not just as a marketing tool, but also as a community building tool. Interact with other businesses by referring clients to them, by asking and answering questions. Facebook is a wonderful opportunity to provide support to your fellow bakeries and local businesses. See what they're doing online and offline, offer ideas and form a community.

Your business page and your personal page should be kept separate. You might support certain political or social causes on your personal page, but your business page should be all about your products and services and include a link back to your website.

Starting a business on a shoestring means marketing through your personal network at first. Facebook is a great way to introduce your business or even your business exploration. Because this powerful tool is used for discovering and maintaining many personal connections, Facebook enables you to reach out first to the people you know and trust. Social networks in general are ideal launching pads because often people will invite you to connect and they want to find out about you. Facebook is a great way to passively introduce your business without being "pushy."

Your network of friends can opt-in to your business page and read as much or as little about you and your business as they wish. Consider inviting other people you already know to join your business/fan page. After you have invited your initial list of contacts, you can increase your fan base "offline" by creating a list of everyone you know. You may be surprised how many people you think of! You will probably have no problem coming up with an initial list of at least one hundred names when you include:

- Your family members - even those whom you see only at weddings and funerals
- Neighbors - include everyone on the address lists of your neighborhood association, your community pool, or Clubhouse
- Friends from church
- Friends from your former jobs
- Friends from your spouse's job
- Parents of your children's friends - use address lists from school, soccer team, gymnastics, Girl Scouts, Boy Scouts, etc.
- Your college roommate's family, friends, and co-workers
- Social clubs
- Sports clubs
- Your family's doctors, dentists, orthodontist, etc.
- Your attorney, insurance agent, etc.

Whenever you meet someone new, add them to your list.

Is Facebook effective?
As an entrepreneur starting a cupcake business, there are only so many hours in a day to accomplish all that you need to do. You want to spend your valuable time on efforts that will yield positive results. Research conducted in 2009 by Rice University suggests that Facebook is worth the effort.

The study, based on surveys of more than 1,700 respondents over a three-month period, found that compared with one bakery's typical customers, the company's Facebook fans:

- Made 36% more visits to their bakery each month.
- Spent 45% more of their eating-out dollars at the bakery.
- Spent 33% more.
- Had 14% higher emotional attachment to the bakery's brand.
- Had 41% greater psychological loyalty toward the bakery.

According to one of the study's authors, the results indicate that Facebook fan pages offer an effective and low-cost way of social-media marketing.

Twitter

Since this is a book about starting a cupcake business and not internet marketing, this section is only an introduction to Twitter within the context of how it can be used to promote your business. If you are already a Twitter user, use this section as a gut check on how effectively you're using it. If you are new to Twitter, make sure you educate yourself more thoroughly about Twitter functionality such as ReTweeting, Hashtags, Direct Messages, Twitter Lists, Location Services and more.

While some may argue that social media is not critical to success, there are too many examples of bakeries that have launched entirely on the internet and then grown into brick and mortar operations. Moreover, there are examples of bakeries across the world that have harnessed social media so successfully that it is a primary marketing channel on par with and sometimes exceeding all other traditional media. There are even stories of bakeries that were on the verge of failure, only to reach out to their online networks to be saved thanks to a viral outpouring of support. For these reasons, social media marketing is prominently included in this book. Twitter can even be used to guide your business plan as you reach out to your network for support.

Twitter Simplified

In a nutshell, Twitter allows you to post short messages on the internet. These messages can be seen not only by other Twitter users and specifically your network of followers, but also by the major search engines that offer a real-time *Twitter* feed on their search results pages. If someone searches for "best cupcakes Nashville" your name should come up not only in traditional search engine results, but also in Twitter real time results. That is, if people are talking about you!

The concept of Twitter is to create a network of people with similar interests. For a cupcake business this might include cupcakes and baking in general, your shop and its products, small business, marketing, baking industry trends, and lastly, your local community. You want to get local users through your door, so connect with them first on Twitter.

The easiest way to start (once you've created an account) is by searching subjects of interest at **search.Twitter.com**. Read the posts of others and follow people who you are interested in. Again, you should follow people in your community as well as people and businesses worldwide. In turn, they can choose to follow you. Often other users will automatically follow you but sometimes they like to read the kind of posts you make, so don't hesitate to start making observations, joining conversations and contributing. By posting and following, you build a network much in the same way you build business and customer connections in the real world. Like Facebook, the more value you add in creating informative posts, the more people will follow you. It seems difficult at first when no one is following you, but surprisingly, people will find you and want to follow you.

How to turn followers into customers? When you post about your business, your community, offer specials and news about your business, it keeps your cupcakes in the minds of potential customers. Thus, the larger your following is, the greater your chances are for bringing in customers. As with Facebook, this is not an excuse to spam. It is a process that builds slowly and must be nurtured.

When you have a physical location, you want to encourage your patrons to follow you on Facebook and Twitter. This can be as simple as mentioning your Facebook and Twitter names in your menu, or in the window of your shop. Likewise, on your website, you want to encourage prospective customers to follow you. Give them a reason. A cupcake shop in Los Angeles posts a daily coupon code on Twitter and gives a free treat to the first 5 people in the door who mention the code. Mobile vendors, including cupcake trucks, use Twitter to post their location for the day and countless bakeries post updates on Twitter when products are fresh out the oven, or if new flavors are offered.

If people are interested in what you write about, they will follow you. An added element of Twitter is direct messaging. Often your followers will send you direct messages. This could be simply to say hello or potentially to request something from you. A small bakery in Charlotte, NC doubled their clientele by finding and following local Twitter users and then invited them to place orders via Twitter. Customers can place an order from their phone or computer and the bakery has the order waiting when they walk through the door.

Why is Twitter so valuable? Research suggests that only 14% of people trust advertisements, while 78% of people trust the advice or recommendations of other consumers. Your brief tweets are distributed both directly to people who have asked to receive information from you and, more importantly, those messages can be passed on with a click of a button to many new potential customers.

Use Twitter to educate customers about your bakery. Engage in the conversations they're having about your neighborhood and establish yourself as someone who cares about the community. Listen to what your customers want. Twitter is a great opportunity to discover new innovations. Twitter enables you to hear what people are saying about your cupcake business. If it is negative, get in there and address the situation. Speak one-to-one with your customers, and show your concern for what they think. In the same light, don't hesitate to thank other users for their praise.

In the early stages of planning your business, Twitter can be a great opportunity to ask people in your community what they want from a cupcake business. Do some sample "testing" of ideas. Figure out what is important – price, novel recipes, locally sourced ingredients, great coffee. Develop relationships with others in the business. And most importantly, give people something to talk about and a reason to buy from you.

Social Food Sites

Each social media property functions as a way to increase your page ranking for your website, reach additional prospective customers, and establish your presence on the web. They all require the same basic information: a small bio about you or your business, a link to a website, and for many of the food-related sites, a photo.

The more of these properties you develop and the greater your presence in the larger food community, the more you will reach potential customers. In addition to Facebook and Twitter, consider these additional websites:

- Yelp (www.yelp.com)
- TasteSpotting (www.tastespotting.com)
- Foodgawker (www.foodgawker.com)

- Squidoo (www.squidoo.com) is one of the most-visited sites in the world. Developing a Squidoo lens for your Internet Marketing efforts is a another way to establish yourself as an expert in a particular subject. This site is very niche oriented. For example, if you create cupcakes in a small community, you could create a cupcake "Guide for Brides" that is tailored to the needs and expectations of clients where you live. You can create a "who is" page and link it back to your website.

Traditional Marketing

To entrench yourself in your community and be the business that comes to mind first when people are looking for cupcakes, there are things you can do to foster good relations in your community whose marketing benefits can't be beat.

Sponsorships

Sponsoring a local community sports club or putting an ad in your local high school's play program each year can add tremendous visibility for very little cost while fostering good will. There are so many different opportunities in this area; you will want to choose one or two that mean something to you and be willing and able to say no. Having an advertising budget to work from can really help keep your decision-making simple.

Chamber of Commerce Membership

For the small membership fee, you get the benefit of not only having a voice in the business decisions that affect your community, but you have unlimited networking possibilities with the business people in your town or community. Being a member of the Chamber of Commerce also gives you access to business resources and supports.

Better Business Bureau

Perhaps even more so with a business in the food industry, but truly in any service industry, membership in the Better Business Bureau can be an invaluable source of developing customer loyalty. Simply by knowing that you are willing to comply by their standards can make your customers more comfortable with you.

Charity Events

While it may seem like marketing is all about spending money, it's really about visibility. You do not have to spend a lot of money to be involved in your community in the ways that really matter. Depending on the size of your town or neighborhood and the reach of your business, you can choose which of the community outreach options fit with your business.

Becoming involved in your local Relay for Life or Race for the Cure Campaign, or helping to raise funds for the March of Dimes or the United Way, can help establish you as a business that cares about more than profits…and that goes a long way toward developing customer loyalty.

Low Cost Marketing Solutions
Business Cards

A low tech but equally important step in marketing your business in a personal and cost effective way is business cards. Not only should you have them, but also you must carry and hand them out on a regular basis.

Carry business cards with you everywhere, and give those cards to everyone with whom you come in contact. Everyone you meet is a potential customer. Your business cards should complement your website design and other marketing materials and be designed with your logo.

Postcards

Postcards can be used to announce your cupcake business and on a regular basis to announce specials or discounts you are offering. While much of our contemporary society is online, direct mail marketing is still one of the most effective ways of reaching your customers. As you develop a client base, you can send targeted postcards that offer special discounts for birthdays, anniversaries, or other special occasions.

Events Marketing

Make a list of where crowds gather in your town. Here is a list to get you started:

- Professional Sporting Events
- Concerts
- Parades
- High School Sporting Event
- Political Rallies
- Parks on Sunny Days
- Shopping Malls
- Dog Shows
- State Parks on weekends

One way to market to crowds is to go to an event with a team of helpers – family, friends, college students or a scout troop looking to raise money — and pass out flyers, postcards or coupons that encourage people to come to your shop. For events with a specific ending time, have your marketing team wait on the sidewalks outside the event as it ends. This is a quick way to reach hundreds of potential customers. Your team should be professional and non-intrusive. This personal contact with potential customers is a great way to introduce yourself to your community and is much less expensive than official sponsorships.

Special Events Facilities

Introduce yourself to special event coordinators at

country clubs, colleges, restaurants, churches, and other facilities that host weddings, rehearsal dinners, and other special events.

LEGAL CONSIDERATIONS

When planning your cupcake business or any food preparation business, you must obviously do your homework on a range of topics. Each state, county, and municipality will have its own regulations, permit, and licensing requirements, and zoning restrictions.

To be a responsible business owner, you need to research the laws and guidelines where your business will be located and take seriously all the responsibilities that come with selling food to the public. You may discover that the lovely space you think is ideal is actually more restrictive and costly to get up to code than another location the next town over. Never let your emotions rule your decision making process when it comes to regulations beyond your control.

With your new business venture will come the legal costs of getting the venture off the ground. You will incur fees ranging from acquiring required licenses and permits to filing fees with the Secretary of State. These charges depend on the business structure you choose to set up and will vary from state to state.

In addition to a visit to your local SCORE office, a consultation with a business attorney in your local area is a smart place to start once you commit to opening a cupcake bakery. This research is part of any start-up. The fees can vary widely, but are typically tax deductable. Ask for referrals from other business owners or check with your Chamber of Commerce when searching for an attorney. You may also wish to call your local bar association because many have a referral service.

Some attorneys may charge a consultation fee of $50 to $500, but in most cases the fee will be applied to any services that you have them perform. The most common service that an attorney will provide is setting up the business type (corporation, LLC, sole proprietorship) that you choose and taking care of all the paperwork associated with keeping you legal.

Your attorney can also provide counsel on the liabilities involved in operating your cupcake business and attempt to insulate you from personal liability. In addition, you may want them to prepare service contracts tailored to your business so that you have recourse in the event that you don't get paid or a dispute arises with a vendor, client or employee.

Business Types

When forming a business, you have several options. A **sole proprietorship** is a business in which you are the sole owner. This type of business can also be called a DBA or "Doing Business As" if you are using a business name rather than your personal name. Legally and for tax purposes, you are not separate from your business; rather you are operating under a different name. You are personally liable for your business and its debt; all income is added to your personal tax returns (pass-through taxation). If you are in the earliest stages of exploration, have no employees and not selling anything, then this type of business is easy to setup, easy to maintain and if you decide not to open a bakery after all, easy to dissolve. If your bakery moves beyond the planning stage, a sole proprietorship offers very little personal asset protection and is not advised.

The second business type is a **partnership** in which there is more than one business owner sharing in the profit and liability incurred by the company. A partnership, however, should be formed into a business that protects the partners involved, such as a **corporation** or **limited liability company** (LLC).

A corporation is a legal entity in which you (or you and your partners) would be members or shareholders. Through the formation of a corporation you will be insulated from personal liability that may occur in the operation of your business. However, keeping up the formalities of a corporation is a time consuming and expensive proposition. A corporation can buy real estate, enter into contracts, sue and be sued completely separately from its owners. Also, money can be raised easier via the sale of stock; its ownership can be transferred via the transfer of stock; and the tax advantages can be considerable (i.e. you are able to deduct many business expenses, healthcare programs, etc. that other legal entities cannot.) If you are investing in something substantial enough to purchase real-estate, raise money by selling shares, offer healthcare to your employees, then a corporation may be appropriate for you.

The most common choice for smaller businesses is the formation of an LLC – limited liability company. With an LLC you will enjoy the same protection from personal liability as you would in a corporation, but you do so without many of the formalities that are usually associated with a full-blown corporation. An LLC also provides easy management and "pass-through" taxation (profits and losses are added to the owner(s) personal tax returns) like a Sole Proprietorship/Partnership. There is an initial cost to establish your LLC and each state charges an annual fee to maintain it. In many states, you must also submit an "annual report" or "statement of information," which is a one-page form sent by the state. Some states also have a flat LLC tax that can range anywhere from $250 to the low thousands.

Organizational Documentation

If you determine that you will be creating an LLC, limited liability partnership or corporation, there are some organizational documents you must file. The easiest way is to use an attorney or an online service such as Legal Zoom.

When you file your organizational documents, the agency (often the Secretary of State) will also check your business name to make sure it does not duplicate one being used by another business. To ensure your application is accepted and to save time, research first with the state filing office to make sure your business name is available. This can often be done online.

Keep in mind that a name may be available to use in your state, but you can still have legal trouble if the name infringes upon the trademark of another business. Simply stated, you can't use a name (or logo, slogan, appearance, signage or product name) that can be easily confused with a competing bakery that has registered that trademark. There were multiple trademark lawsuit threats by the famous California cupcake bakery "Sprinkles."

From the <u>LA Times</u>: *Lawyers for Sprinkles said, they have sent about a dozen similar letters to shops around the country and filed three lawsuits, including one last month against Famous Cupcakes in North Hollywood for using dots in its packaging and throughout the store...The trademarked "modern dot," a circle-in-a-circle piece of candy that sits atop every Sprinkles cupcake, helps eaters tell the difference between flavors like lemon coconut and red velvet.*

Even if they have not registered a trademark, an existing business is protected by unfair competition laws. For example, if you select the name Awesome Cupcakes and there is a bakery in your community called Awesome Bakery, you could be subject to a trademark infringement or an unfair competition suit. Even though the names are unique and the word *Awesome* is common, the fact that both businesses sell baked goods could cause customer confusion. Selecting a name that is not only available in your state, has an available URL, and has a very low likelihood of causing any customer confusion takes time to research but will avoid legal trouble down the road.

Business Name Registration

If you choose to present yourself under any name other than your proper legal name, you will have to register your fictitious business name. This is handled typically at the county level. First, conduct a search through the county database (usually online) to make sure the name is not already in use. Then, there is a simple form to fill out and a fee (anywhere from $10 to $100). Some states may have other requirements such as publishing the notification in a local newspaper classifieds. Your county clerk's office will provide the details about the process in your area.

Tax Considerations

As a business owner, you may be required to collect taxes on goods sold in your cupcake shop. This is a complex matter that should be addressed by consulting your accountant. The tax laws that govern your business depend on the kinds of items you offer, how they are served, and how they are consumed. Moreover, they are frequently changing.

For example, in California, tax generally applies to sales of food and beverages if those items are served for consumption at your place of business. You are considered to have a place of business where customers consume their purchases if you provide tables and chairs or counters for dining, or provide trays, glasses, dishes, or other tableware; however, sales of hot bakery goods are not taxable when sold to go, unless they are sold as part of a combination package. You can see this is tricky! In just this one state's example, there are different rules based entirely on how the food is ordered and consumed.

By consulting an accountant, attorney, or even looking into your state and local requirements, you can determine whether there is a state sales tax or another type of tax that you must collect in the course of your business. Working with your local SCORE office is the best free way to explore your tax liability as they have assisted thousands of local entrepreneurs and know the ins and outs of your specific community.

As a starting point, a complete listing of states' departments of revenue are listed at taxadmin.org/fta/link/.

Tax ID's

A federal ID number, called an FEIN or EIN is like your personal Social Security number, except it is for your business. This number is used by the government to identify your business and you will use it over and over on many of your business documents. You need an EIN to open a business bank account, apply for business licenses, and filing a tax return. The name "employee identification number" is confusing because even if you don't have, or don't plan to have employees, EIN's are required for most businesses. The exception is if you are a sole proprietorships with no employees. Then, you can use your social security number as your identification. Partnerships, LLC's and corporations need an EIN whether they have employees or not.

Obtaining an employer's ID number is as simple as using the IRS online form called "EIN Assistant". Once you complete the form, the number is assigned to you immediately and becomes part of your IRS record (for paying taxes) within two weeks. Note, LLC's must file their organizational documents before applying for an EIN.

Employment tax

If you have employees, it is your responsibility to withhold taxes from their paycheck, keep track the amounts you are withholding and make regular payments to the state and federal government. These taxes include federal income tax withholding, social security and Medicare taxes, and Federal Unemployment Tax Act (FUTA) taxes. **http://tinyurl.com/bakery21**

This may seem intimidating if you've never done it, but like anything else, it gets easier after a few times. Most entrepreneurs choose to manage this complexity by hiring a part-time bookkeeper and/or using an integrated bookkeeping/payroll software solution. Probably the best-known of these is Quickbooks. An accounting package simplifies the painstaking process of making calculations, completing reports and writing and signing checks.

Tax Exemption

A seller's permit, also known as a Certificate of Authority or a Resale Certificate exempts you from paying sales tax on some of your purchases including ingredients or anything that you resell. Handy when you buy items in bulk! Keep excellent records so the IRS doesn't think you're taking advantage of this benefit. The items you purchase without paying sales tax must be used solely for your business, not personal use. A state sales tax exemption can save you money by allowing you to purchase your products wholesale. Wholesale vendors usually require a copy of this certificate or the number in order to set up a wholesale account.

Most states provide the form online through the state tax department, but your local chamber of commerce should also have the information you need. However, once you've applied for a tax exempt certificate, you will be expected to start filing monthly or quarterly sales tax reports in most states.

Business Permits and Licensing

Before opening for business, you will be required to secure a food establishment permit from your state, county or city health department. The cost of the permit is minor while the preparation and expense to meet the requirement can be costly. Permits are required for permanent locations as well as temporary operations such as a kiosk, mobile truck, or marketplace. If, for example, you bake cupcakes in a commercial kitchen to sell in a mobile vending business, both the kitchen and the truck will be inspected.

Health inspectors might seem intimidating to novice or unprepared business owners, but in fact, they are a great resource. While their job is ultimately to protect the community, in doing so, they protect you. Inspectors want to make sure that all areas of your bakery meet the legal standards set by your community. Since most municipalities are burdened by layers of bureaucracy, the health inspector can help you traverse the red tape and give you the information about the requirements you'll have to meet.

In a health inspection, your inspector will be checking to see the cleanliness of the operation including utensils, equipment, and surfaces; how food is stored, prepared and displayed; employee heath and hygiene; the design and installation of equipment; organization of storage; cleanliness of restrooms; and the materials and construction of your overall facilities. The biggest concern of the health inspector is PHF or potentially hazardous food. Potentially hazardous food is primarily defined in terms of whether or not it requires time/temperature control for safety to limit pathogen growth or toxin formation. For example, with cupcakes, consider the use of egg and dairy products and the potential of food borne illness resulting from inaccurate heating/cooling, cross contamination, packaging, storage, etc. Most states require at least one employee to have completed a food safety training course and be present at the time of inspection.

Prior to your opening day you will be inspected. If your initial inspection results in any faults, you must correct them before the permit will be issued. Because a major problem could result in significant delay and expense, you should bring the health department into your planning process from the outset. For example, you don't want to invest in an opening day event only to find the grease trap you've installed is too small. Moreover, if you've been given a rent allowance from your landlord, you don't want any surprises that will delay your opening, and have to start paying rent without bringing in revenue. If you work with the health department from the outset in a spirit of cooperation most inspection faults (if any) will be minor.

Health departments will perform periodic inspections – both scheduled and surprise—on an on-going basis. The focus of these inspections is on critical risk violations, which are those violations most likely to contribute to food borne illness. Critical areas of focus will be safe food temperatures, employee practices such as hand washing, and an adequately supplied bathroom; the absence of vermin (immediate risks: rodents, cockroaches, flies); water and sanitation, including having enough hot water; the presence of a sewage disposal system. A sample inspection checklist is included with the bonus resource items on our website.

Reinspections are performed as a follow-up to a routine inspection that results in written orders. Only violations not in compliance from the initial inspection will be shown on the reinspection report. If all violations are in compliance at reinspection, the report will state "no violations to report."

106

Once you've passed your first health inspection, teach your employees to operate your business in a manner that prioritizes health and safety. This will ensure that unannounced inspections are never an issue and that the public can be confident in patronizing your cupcake business.

Listed are a few things to keep in mind while you are being inspected:

Greet the inspector. Be calm, communicative and remember that you are working with the inspector to keep your bakery safe and customers healthy.

Do not refuse an inspection. Refusing an inspection creates an antagonistic relationship between you and the heath department for a long time. Rest assured that upon return with an inspection warrant you will be penalized for every infraction, no matter how minor.

Be friendly, but not overly social. Do not offer anything to your inspector, including food, coffee, water, etc. It is important to maintain a professional relationship with your health inspector and this is not a social call. More importantly, it can be seen as a bribe.

Walk and talk with the inspector. Accompanying the inspector shows your interest in food safety and allows you to know the details of any violation.

Take notes. This gives you something to reference when addressing violations or planning further employee training.

Ask questions. If you do not understand why something is a violation, ask. The inspector will explain what portion of the food code it violates and the proper solution. Try not to be confrontational as it breaks down communication.

Do not take it personally. Nobody is perfect, and mistakes happen. Rather than dwelling on every violation the inspector finds, correct the mistakes and strive for a better inspection the next time around.

Fix critical violations on the spot. Critical violations are those directly related to food borne illnesses. If they are not corrected immediately, your customers can become sick. For violations that cannot be remedied on the spot, set a time frame for correction; the inspector will most likely perform a follow-up inspection for critical violations that require more time for correction.

Know your stuff. Inspectors often quiz managers and employees alike to gauge their knowledge of food safety and preparation processes. All owners and managers must have up-to-date training. In some counties, lack of food safety knowledge is a critical violation and can shut down a business.

Have records on hand. The inspector will ask for all of your records regarding food safety management. These can include temperature check records, receiving logs and employee illnesses. Also, the inspector will ask to see your operators permit to make sure it is current.

Something to remember
Part of a health inspector's job is education. If your facility is lacking in a specific area of safe food handling, arrange a date and time for the inspector to return and give your employees a food safety lesson. This will help assure that your customers and employees have a healthy, enjoyable experience in your establishment.

In the appendix of this book and on our website, you will find a list of contact information for each state's regulatory agency as well as a common checklist for health inspections. As a food service provider to your community, you should take your state's regulations, community's zoning regulations, and the liability aspects of owning a business very seriously. If you do not, you can face serious consequences, including fines, lawsuits, and the loss of your business.

While this book is intended to be a guide to help you understand the process of opening your own cupcake business, only your attorney can assist you and give you a thorough explanation of what legal forms are required in your community.

The following is a list of standard equipment and conditions that are most often required from the heath department. When scouting locations or planning build-outs keep these items in mind as they may be unexpected expenses:

- 3-compartment sink with a grease trap installed
- Hand sink
- Low Radiation Lights that are covered
- Washable surfaces - walls, floors, cabinets, counter tops that do not retain flour, dirt and dust.
- Ceiling must be of non-absorbent material
- Separate refrigerator, freezer
- Storage for equipment - pans, spatulas, bowls, etc.
- Foodsafe storage for ingredients
- Adequate storage space for ingredients
- Approved water source

Insurance

This is probably the most important area of business ownership that is almost always overlooked at the outset. For those branching out from a home business, you may have simply been able to add an addendum to your homeowner's policy, but when you step into the commercial side, having the right kind of insurance is vital.

General Liability Coverage

109

Liability insurance has several parts, all designed to protect you from loss when catastrophe strikes. The types of liability insurance you need to consider include coverage for property damage, loss of use, personal injury, and special insurance that protects you against claims arising from raw materials you use in the creation of your products.

You want to be protected from the unthinkable. Imagine your worst nightmare come true about your business, and you will understand the importance of liability insurance.

Consult with your attorney to determine the type of coverage you need and don't be afraid to shop around. One warning: the cheapest insurance coverage is not always the best choice. You want coverage that comes with real protection, great service in case you have to file a claim, and an agent who can help you navigate the insurance industry successfully.

The standard liability coverage for a cupcake shop ranges from $1,000,000 to $5,000,000, depending on the size and scope of your business. Coverage should include product liability protection. For example, you use cherries as an ingredient in your cupcakes and the cherries are recalled. Even though your supplier and the manufacturer of the cherries are likely liable, a customer who gets sick eating your product can still sue or try to sue you, so having protection for product liability is critical.

Business Interruption Coverage

You should consider business interruption insurance and loss-of-use insurance, which protects you in the case that you are unable to continue using the location of your business because of damage from fire or flood, or from theft, vandalism, or closed roads.

You can base your coverage on what you would need to survive (fixed costs plus income) for up to six months.

Don't assume your coverage has everything you need; talk to your agent and read your policy carefully. Add coverage where you think you need it.

Property Coverage

This type of policy covers business personal property, including machinery, cooking equipment, ovens, point-of-sale systems and stock. If you are renting, your landlord will likely require you to maintain a certain level of property insurance. Even if the lease indicates the landlord has a property insurance policy, you want to rely on your own individual insurance coverages. This will prevent litigation between you and the landlord should there be a claim.

Workers Compensation

Workers' compensation benefits provide coverage for medical expenses as well as reimbursement for lost wages when employees are injured on the job. Because some baking processes can be hazardous, it is more common for a bakery employee, than say, an office worker, to be injured on the job. The employers' liability portion of most Workers' Compensation policies protects your company in the event that an employee files suit claiming that your negligence was the cause of the work related illness or injury. Workers' Compensation insurance is required in many states. There are multiple ways to purchase workers compensation, so it is best to consult your state for the regulations that affect you: http://tinyurl.com/bakery20

Equipment Breakdown and Miscellaneous Equipment Coverage

As well, you should have insurance to cover your equipment (base it on the cost of replacing, not repairing the equipment). This type of policy protects against damage caused by power surges, mechanical breakdown, motor burnout, and boiler damage. Some of the equipment in your bakery can cost five figures. You don't want to have to replace a vital 20-quart mixer or double convection oven without insurance.

Spoilage Coverage
One of the issues that bakeries face is food spoilage or food contamination as a result of equipment failure. Imagine the liability if a refrigerator full of cupcakes for a wedding broke down due to a power surge or motor burnout. While the **Equipment Breakdown** policy covers the refrigerator, it won't cover the food inside or the loss of income if you can't sell that product.

Other policies to ask your provider about:

Business Auto Coverage
You need commercial auto coverage if you or your employees will use titled vehicles in their work. Examples include making deliveries or picking up supplies.

Business Umbrella
An Umbrella Liability provides coverage for claims that exceed the amount of coverage on your General Liability policy and may also add coverage to your Commercial Auto coverage as well as the Employers' Liability coverage on your Workers' Compensation policy. When claims are in excess of your other policies, this kicks in.

Business Crime Coverage
The primary crime for bakeries is employee theft of inventory. Other similar exposures may be present if retail and wholesale operations are conducted. Internet sales may create additional exposures such as identity theft or scams.

LOCATION, LOCATION, LOCATION

Unless you are a famous cupcake shop that people will drive for miles to experience, location matters. It is very rare, however, for location to be secondary to product reputation. Your chances for success grow exponentially when your business is visible and accessible. When you start this process, it is likely that you find a building or location for your shop that is not ideal. While the price might seem great or the décor adorable, walk away if the space has been a string of business failures. No matter how urgent your goals, never rush into a location if it isn't ideal. There will always be another space that's even better than the first.

The closer you are to a community center, the more visible and accessible you will be. Cupcake bakeries succeed when they are located in high traffic, visible locations with lots of residential families in the surrounding neighborhoods.

The most important factor in choosing location is access. As you will read in the following case study, without good access you simply cannot thrive no matter how great your products and services are. Never choose a location without trying to drive to it from multiple directions and analyzing the difficulties your customers might encounter.

Case Study

Company: **Bakery Basket**
Location: **Boise, Idaho**

Bakery Basket was a very popular bakery in West Boise. They marketed themselves as an old-fashioned bakery and offered seating for up to 90 eat-in guests. They served specialty coffees in addition to their sweet treats, and offered a small but delicious selection of lunch sandwiches. The reviews of the bakery from customers were always four and five star. Comments from customers included:

"Family owned, clean and all is made fresh, not frozen products like others. Great sit down area, with good service."

"Bakery Basket has made many items for me to bring into work, from pies, rolls and cakes to cookies and everything in between. Their products are fresh; the frosting is not that over sweet gooey stuff you get at large chains, it is velvet soft and good.

You pay a little more but you also get better ingredients and to me it is well worth it. They are located in a good area of Boise. Stop in and try them!! You will not be disappointed."

Bakery Basket was a small, family-owned bakery that offered specialty temptations like éclairs and fresh muffins along with a wide variety of donuts, bagels, and cookies. They offered special services like made-to-order birthday cakes with a special recipe butter cream frosting and also made wedding cakes.

They were enormously popular, but made one bad decision that resulted in them going out of business after only a few years: they were in a location that was incredibly difficult to access.

In order to get to the parking lot, cars either had to cut through a gas station parking lot or go around a corner and turn in to a doctor's office parking lot and cut through the other side of the gas station. The bakery did not have its own direct access from the street.

Worse yet, the location was hidden behind other businesses with no visible signage from the road. The final straw appeared to be a median in the road that did not allow incoming traffic to turn left into the gas station and bakery.

It did not matter how delectable their products were or how inviting their dine-in area was. Not enough people were able to find them to continue generating enough revenue.

Shortly after Bakery Basket went out of business, the entire area was torn out and reconstructed to be more accessible, but the median preventing left turns has still caused difficulty.

Bakery Basket's story demonstrates the ultimate importance of location. You can do everything else right, but if you are in the wrong location, you will still add an uncontrollable risk component to your ability to stay in business.

Choosing Your Location

Often aspiring business owners dream of owning a shop and scout locations they think would be ideal. Rather than waiting until space opens up in your coveted location, start doing an evaluation of the site's suitability now. Too often people make decisions based on emotion and ultimately choose a location for the wrong reasons.

Armed with comprehensive information such as demographic data, present and planned transportation routes, city and downtown land uses, municipal restrictions and other related factors, you will be able to make a decision based on facts rather than assumptions.

When considering a site for a new cupcake shop, you must determine the market you are after and attempt to locate in a place most convenient to that population. The demographic who does most of the cupcake buying in the U.S. is women. A bakery is ideal in a shopping center or strip mall located near a neighborhood, but only if that shopping center is anchored with a grocery store. If it is anchored with something like a hardware store or clothing store, your demographic won't be thinking food when they drive/walk by. A cupcake bakery might also be located adjacent to or in some cases even on a college campus because a major segment of the market is found in nearby dormitories, fraternities, and sororities. An office complex might work if there is sufficient foot traffic from nearby office buildings and if the shop has adequate visibility. Don't limit your imagining to a single location. Consider opportunities in the following settings:

* Residential areas
* Central trade areas
* Shopping centers
* Recreation areas
* Education facilities
* Other attractions

In addition to general areas for locating a cupcake shop, you also want to think more specifically about the neighborhood and the clientele you want to attract. Knowing the median income, ethnic make-up, site availability, competition, existing businesses, and growth patterns assures that you don't make an obvious mistake. While one kind of concept could thrive in one part of town, it could fail in another based on perceived price, authenticity, cultural relevance and taste in another part of town. The Bureau of Census and the Department of Commerce provide detailed data on neighborhood make-up.

In some cases there are real-estate opportunities that

116

are desired because of the long-established patterns of success, trendiness or growth. In Saratoga Springs, New York for example, businesses long for storefront openings on Broadway Ave. Aspiring business owners must have the business plan to ensure the return on investment of a higher rent will enable them to meet their obligations and make a profit. Some locations are so exclusive or otherwise desirable that retail space is not available or priced beyond the rate at which your business will still be profitable. If no site is available or existing sites are priced too high, there is no alternative but to look elsewhere.

Conducting your own research will prepare you to make a sound selection. Traffic studies can be obtained from the broker managing the prospective building and for less than $100 you can get a site demographic analysis online with a breakdown of the location you are contemplating and the income levels of the surrounding area. The following is a complete breakdown of variables to consider when selecting a location:

Locale
Type of neighborhood- urban, suburban, etc.
Customer profile criteria
Other types of businesses in neighborhood
Pattern of growth
New construction or remodeling underway

Appropriate Zoning and Codes
Bakery specifically allowed
Parking space(s) criteria
Use permits
Curb breaks
Food service requirements

Competition
Total number of cupcake shops
Total number of dessert shops (ice-cream, cookies)
Total number of bakeries selling similarly priced items

117

Total number of seats in each category
Level of service
New competition under construction or planned

Specific Lot Characteristics
Clear title or lease considerations
Adequate parking, square footage determined
Landscaping and other features

Traffic Arteries
Traffic counts
Street patterns and flow direction
Number of lanes
Surface type and condition
Curbs and sidewalks
Type and quality of lighting
Ingress/egress to site
Obstacles and hazards
Public transportation
Distance(s) from intersections, transit, terminals,
landmarks
Other characteristics

Utilities and Municipal Services
Electricity
Gas
Other energy source(s)
Water
Sewers
Police protection
Fire protection
Hydrant(s) existing or proposed
Trash collection
High speed internet

Visibility
Driving

Walking
Degree of obstruction
Sign location and height

Cost Data
Cost per square foot
Site Improvement cost(s)
Taxes

When you've identified a few locations that seem like they will work for you, it's a good idea to spend time "stalking" each location. Become familiar with the type of clientele the location draws. Look at the parking lot. Walk through the existing shops as a customer. See if your vision of your cupcake business fits with the feel of the location.

Contact the broker or landlord to see the inside of your potential space. Make note of things like electrical and plumbing (for most large ovens, you will need to have 220). How much effort will be involved in making the location ready for your business? Will the space be large enough to accommodate growth? Is there enough storage? Is there a dedicated delivery area?

Which Corner
If you are considering a retail operation in a shopping center location, there is no doubt that a sidewalk accessible space is often the most ideal location. Consistent foot-traffic is important to a steady sales flow. This is one of the reasons cupcake bakeries have flourished. People pick them up on the way to work for an office party, at lunch for dessert, and on the way home for an evening treat or an after work event. Cupcakes don't require a special event and yet they are suitable for the finest of wedding receptions.

You should also consider the visibility factors of the location. Is your building visible from the street? Will traffic be able to see your store sign? Does the shopping center offer additional centerpost signage for added visibility?

Zoning Codes
Before leasing a site, take the time to check with the municipality's planning and zoning commission, or whoever controls land use to insure that the prospective cupcake business can be opened. Because entrepreneurs often envision our community differently than our local governments, we often see opportunity in places that are not (but could be) zoned for food establishments.

An example of this type of restriction that is quite common is a local ordinance that requires a minimum number of off-street parking places for all food establishments regardless of size. Parking is just one example of the many restrictions that prevent or seriously delay the opening of a brick and mortar shop. Sign codes, use permits, building and lot requirements, curb breaks must be explored before signing a lease.

Once you have narrowed down your location prospects, you can move on to the other considerations, like landlords, leases, and costs.

What Makes a Good Landlord?
The best way to determine whether or not a landlord is going to meet your needs is to talk to the other tenants. You'll likely hear all the horror stories. They'll fill your ear with all the gossip, but you'll also find out if the landlord is pretty good at getting repairs done and keeps the lot clean and doesn't gouge you on lease renewals.

In addition to talking to the tenants, you can check with the Better Business Bureau and push the leasing agent to allow you the opportunity to speak directly with the landlord if you have additional questions.

Some things you may want to consider asking the landlord are:

1. Is there a tenant association?
2. Do you have promos that you pay for, like sidewalk sales?
3. Since in most situations the first two answers will be no, the next question may be if you can organize your own promotional opportunities for the shopping site.
4. Ask about conditions at different times of year. Are there snow removal problems? Vandalism issues? Special security requirements?

Be sure to shop carefully for your location, because you'll often be obligated to the location for at least the minimum lease term (two years or more), whether you are able to stay in business or not.

Lease Negotiations

When you are negotiating your lease, there are several things you need to understand. How much leverage you have in the negotiating process depends on how desperate the landlord is to get a tenant. If you are opening your business in a community or location where there are several other people wanting the same spot, your landlord will have the upper hand. If, however, you are after a spot that has been sitting empty or you have five other loca tions you can choose from, you are in a great position to bargain.

Before beginning the negotiations, you should check with the trade association (such as the American Bakers Association, www. americanbakers.org) about the industry standard for lease costs as a percentage of income. For example, if the gross income is $200,000 per year, and the industry standard is 13%, your total occupancy costs should be no more than $26,000 per year. (Of course this will vary, based on location, so check your Chamber of Commerce for local adjustments of this variable.)

Remember, occupancy costs include both the rent

portion of your lease plus additional costs like your percentage of utilities, insurance, and maintenance. When negotiating the lease with a landlord, you should not be willing to exceed the industry standard.

Tenant Finish Allowance

Another consideration, and possibly the most important consideration if you are converting an existing building that has not served as a bakery before, is the tenant finish allowance. When negotiating your lease, this is a concession that should be given by the landlord for remaking the building to be used for your business. It is usually negotiated in dollar per square foot. For example, if your landlord offers you $10 per square foot and you are leasing 1,500 square feet, you would have $15,000 to finish the space and make it ready to use for your business.

In most cases, the landlord actually has funds set aside for this purpose and can pay your contractors directly, limiting the amount of cash you have to have available to get started. However, there are certain items, like the oven or HVAC system that the landlord will not cover in the tenant finish allowance.

You should be able to negotiate upgraded air conditioning, new flooring and counters, the removal of all the items being torn out, and other appearance improvements. If your landlord is not able to offer a tenant finish allowance, you may be able to negotiate free rent for the first two to four months in exchange for making the improvements yourself.

Lease Term

Unless you are an established business with a good business credit history, do not expect the lease term to be longer than a few years. The landlord will be taking a greater risk on you as a new business and will therefore keep the term shorter and charge you more in rent than the anchor store would be charged per square foot (anchor stores are not profitable for landlords, but strip malls and shopping centers simply cannot survive without them).

If you go out of business before the lease is up, you still have to pay the lease, and the landlord has a lien against your property in the building as security.

Personal Guarantee

If the landlord requires you to sign a personal guarantee for the lease, this makes it possible for the landlord to go after your personal assets if the business closes. You should try to avoid this if possible, but if you choose to sign a personal guarantee, limit the liability, for example, to stocks and bonds but not your personal home or bank account. This is an unusual situation and should be a last resort, for example, if the space is in great demand. Otherwise, there are usually other location opportunities that do not put your personal finances in jeopardy.

Bargaining Points

Try to get your landlord to agree to limit the amount of increases when you renew your lease. In some cases, you can pin the increase to economic conditions or revenue. Escalations are often tied to a known method of calculation, such as cost-of-living index.

You can also negotiate a discount on rent if you can pay a few months at once, such as paying three months' rent up front and getting one month free.

Options

When negotiating your lease, get plenty of options from your landlord (to renew the lease) to ensure you have the space available if you need it. Longer-term leases are cheaper but difficult to get when you are newly established and have no credit. Be prepared for your options to come with a market adjustment for the cost of the lease, but try to negotiate the lowest possible terms you can.

123

Costs to Consider Beyond the Lease

When opening a cupcake business, you need to be aware of the many additional costs to consider beyond the lease. It usually takes about three times as much cash to open a business as people expect it to take. It is important to do your homework and know how much you are going to need. There are loans available through the Small Business Association that can help.

Signage

A good sign promoting your business and adding visibility is crucial to your success. Signs can cost $5-$10,000, so budget early for this necessary cost. While it's not often, you might be able to negotiate the cost of the sign as a concession from your landlord.

The Grease Trap

Grease traps are expensive to install and difficult to manage. Ideally, you will find a location where the landlord already has a greasetrap, which would make the location advantageous. If you have to install a grease trap, it can be an expensive start-up cost, about $10,000, to install.

CAM

"CAM" stands for common area maintenance, which includes some shared utilities, landscaping, maintenance, and other costs. This cost will be in addition to your lease amount each month, so be sure you talk to the landlord about the cost and budget for it.

Deposits

If you set up new utilities such as a new phone line for your business or you lease credit card processing equipment, a deposit will be required.

Leasing Checklist

Leasing a commercial space instead of purchasing commercial real estate is a smart move for a cupcake business with no track record. While your confidence is high, you must be realistic that there is a chance for failure. Buying a building is a potentially far greater risk than leasing. Unfortunately, there are fewer tenant protections and no standard lease agreements. You'll need a lawyer's help to negotiate the best deal on a commercial lease.

Every commercial lease should be in writing and should include the following details:

- **The rent.** including any increases (called escalations). You'll want to know the going rate for space in the neighborhood before you begin negotiating. It also helps to let the landlord make the first offer, and ask for a lower rent than you think you can initially get.   When there is an economic downturn and businesses are closing, leases obviously drop. Accordingly, when there is a surge in demand for desirable locations, rents rise.
- **The term.** How long the lease runs, when it begins, and under what conditions you can renew the lease. A shorter lease means less commitment, but less predictability for the long run and potentially higher rents. Since location is very important for a cupcake business you may want to opt for a longer lease. You can always attempt to renegotiate lower rents or improvements as time goes on.
- **Utilities.** Whether your rent includes utilities, such as phone, electricity, and water, or whether you'll be charged for these items separately.
- **Fees.** Whether you'll be responsible for paying any of the landlord's maintenance expenses, property taxes, or insurance costs, and if so, how they'll be calculated.

- **Deposits.** Any required deposit and whether you can use a letter of credit instead of cash.
- **Description**. A description of the space you're renting, square footage, available parking, and other amenities.
- **Build Out/Improvements**. A detailed listing of any improvements the landlord will make to the space before you move in. Your landlord may be more willing to make lots of expensive improvements if you're signing a longer lease.
- **Representations.** Any representations made to you by the landlord or leasing agent, such as amount of foot traffic, average utility costs, restrictions on the landlord renting to competitors (such as in a shopping mall), compliance with Americans With Disabilities Act requirements, and so forth. These may come in handy later when you want to renegotiate your lease.
- **Assurances.** That the space is zoned appropriately for a cupcake business/bakery. Of course, you'll also want to check out this information with local zoning authorities.
- **Sublease.** Whether you'll be able to sublease or assign the lease to someone else, and if so, under what conditions. You'll want to negotiate the ability to sublease so that you can move with as little financial pain as possible.
- **Termination.** How either you or the landlord can terminate the lease and the consequences.

When it is time to renegotiate your commercial lease, you'll want to document your reasons for a lower rent or more space improvements with hard facts regarding lower foot traffic than represented, a downturn in your industry, and so forth. Some landlords will even be willing to take a percentage of your sales instead of a flat rental fee when economic times are slow.

As a tenant, you have far more leeway when negotiating a commercial lease rather than with a residential lease, which is one reason why having your own lawyer to represent you in negotiations is so important. A lawyer can also research zoning laws and local ordinances and fill you in on the local real estate market conditions and customs.

FOOD SAFETY

To be successful in any food related business, one must produce items that are safe and wholesome. The production of safe foods is your responsibility. Time and temperature abuse of foods contaminated with food-borne pathogens will certainly lead to a food-borne outbreak that will likely destroy your reputation and business. If anyone gets sick after eating your cupcakes, you may also find doctor bills or worse, a lawsuit on your hands. While this is the reason you have liability insurance, your reputation is far more difficult to recover. These problems can be avoided if you follow safe food handling practices. Be obsessive about food safety! While the incidents are rare, they do happen and can be devastating.

Most jurisdictions require that you have a Food Manager's Certificate to make food for pubic consumption. This might also be called a Food Safety or Food Sanitation permit. The regulating health agency in your community wants to make sure you're educated in proper sanitary practices.

An example of a food safety program is ServSafe offered by the National Restaurant Association Educational Foundation, and provides state-by-state regulations and guidance. You can visit their website at http://www.servsafe.com/Foodsafety/. Another helpful organization for food safety is the American Bakers Association (www.americanbakers.org).

According to the ABA, extra attention needs to be paid to food defenses, allergen controls, and sanitation. Because of the Bioterrorism Act, there are regulations that govern how vigilant you must be about your ingredient sources.

Even though smaller bakeries and cupcake shops are not required to maintain the same level of security as a wholesale distributor, developing clear food safety policies can protect you from risk and reduce the likelihood of introducing any kind of contaminants to your customers.

A food safety issue that needs to be clearly addressed is the control of allergens. Having good cleaning and sanitation processes that help to remove allergens from equipment can help reduce the risk. In addition to maintaining good sanitation habits, you should offer any employees regular monthly training on food safety and sanitation issues. Offer incentives to your employees for completing food safety training and make regular safety presentations part of your business culture.

When developing policies and procedures to handle food safety issues, address the following:
- Store potentially hazardous foods, such as eggs and milk, immediately in the refrigerator (33 to 40°F).
- Purchase high-quality foods from a reliable vendor. The food should be in good condition with the packaging intact, fresh (not beyond expiration date), and at the proper temperature.
- Dry staples should be stored at 50 to 70°F.
- Practice First-in-First-Out (FIFO) to insure safety and quality of your items.
- Ideally, frozen foods should be thawed in the refrigerator 18 to 24 hours prior to preparation. However,

thawing under cold running water (<70°F), in the microwave, or extending the cooking time are all acceptable methods for thawing food.

- Practice good personal hygiene when preparing and handling food. Wash hands before food preparation, after handling raw foods, after using the restroom or at any time the hands become soiled.
- Take measures to prevent cross-contamination if you cook any other food in the same space where you bake and decorate cupcakes.
- Clean and sanitize food contact surfaces such as counter tops, cutting boards, equipment and utensils. One tablespoon of bleach per gallon of water is an effective sanitizing agent.
- Wash fresh fruit thoroughly under cold running water. In refrigerator storage, make sure fresh fruits are wrapped or stored in containers.
- Wear clean clothes and aprons when preparing food.
- Do not use the same towel to wipe food contact surfaces that you use for wiping hands.
- Clean storage and kitchen areas regularly.
- Practice good housekeeping and implement a pest control program for eliminating the spread of disease.

HACCP

Hazard Analysis and Critical Control Point (HACCP) is a food safety approach that can help you develop policies and procedures that address the physical, chemical, and biological hazards that can affect the safety and quality of your food. The focus of an HACCP protocol is on developing prevention measures rather than reactionary measures for food safety.

HACCP is an internationally recognized food safety protocol. Because foodborne illness is something that can significantly harm your clientele, even though smaller bakeries are not required to have HACCP procedures, the additional focus you place on preventing unsafe food handling practices from occurring, the better you mitigate your risk as a business owner.

The National Restaurant Association has estimated that a single incident of food poisoning can cost your business $75,000. For many small cupcake shops, one incident could cost enough to seriously damage your business. To make it easier to develop an effective food safety management program, the state of Alaska has developed a free Active Managerial Control program at http://www.dec.state.ak.us/eh/fss/amc/amcbroch.htm that you can download.

This interactive program can help you develop your food safety protocols by creating customizable Standard Operating Procedures and checklists. A solid HACCP protocol will include the requirement of a Certified Food Protection Manager, ample food safety training for all employees, written and well maintained SOPs, and ongoing monitoring and correction of your food safety system.

9

INGREDIENTS FOR SUCCESS

Designing Your Space

A well designed space can transform your cupcake shop from something ordinary to wonderfully inviting — and make a good impression when your customers walk through the door, enticing them to stay, browse and buy. What is your concept? Clarify your concept and put all the proposed choices from décor to lighting--in writing. If you can't write about them, then they aren't clear enough. When something is crystal clear in your mind, you can express it succinctly and you will save time and money when it comes time to putting those ideas into an actual bakery space.

If you have the financial wherewithal, you can hire a professional space designer to help you maximize the space. Your designer can work directly with your contractors to design a space that works for you. If you cannot afford to hire a designer, you can still make the most of your space with bright lights, open space, and a clean design.

If you do hire a designer, he or she will want to know the exact square footage of the space you have available and should provide you with a CAD design for approval. Always ask to see photos of their other design work, verify their license and certifications, and check references.

Lighting

It all starts with good lighting. You need bright, welcoming lights to make your shop inviting. When your customers walk through the door, there should be attractive display cases that show off your cupcakes. The cases and the space itself should both have bright lighting.

If you have a dine-in area, you can add charm and personality by using decorative lamps. Make sure you train employees to clean the lamps and light fixtures regularly and immediately replace burned or flickering bulbs.

Displays

The first thing you need to determine is whether or not you need cold displays or just simple glass display cases. Regardless of the type of display that you need, you want to maximize the display space and enhance the displays with lighting.

A trick to help make your selections look more delectable and the entire array look more inviting is to choose displays with mirrored backs. Not only do they reflect the light, but they give additional views of your cupcakes.

If you offer wedding cupcakes or other custom-mades, you should also keep a portfolio in the form of a three-ring binder with high-quality photos in plastic sleeves that your customers can look at. Not only will you be demonstrating your skill and ability, but looking at the pictures can help your customers make up their minds about what they want to order.

Counter Space

The tops of your display cases might be the perfect area

for your counter, but they might be glass topped so that customers can see more of what you have available. Regardless of your design choice, you will want ample counter space both for customers and behind the counter for employees to prepare and package orders.

The counters should be spotlessly clean and clear of clutter. There should be space at the cash register for your latest marketing materials (business cards, post cards, flyers advertising specials) as well as room for purchasers to make payment.

Kitchen Design

The design of your kitchen will depend on the scale of your operation and the equipment you require to create your cupcakes. Try to think long-term as shortsighted planning now may cost you dearly. Use the following questions to help you plan:

- Will you make your cupcakes from scratch or from a mix?
- Will you offer any cupcakes that use frozen goods such as fruit?
- Will all of your batches go straight to the front of the shop/foodservice area for sale or will some items be refrigerated?
- Will you cater events or will all of your cupcakes be consumed/sold on site?
- Will you produce recipes that require significant wait times between production stages?
- Will you offer cupcakes that require special preparation environments such as gluten free or vegan?

When designing the space, also think of safety and legal requirements. For example, you will need a separate mop sink, a separate hand washing sink, and a three-compartment sink for washing equipment and dishes.

Will your workspaces be wide enough to prevent accidental damage when a delivery trolley comes rolling through?

You may want to create a quiet space for your office off the kitchen for the inevitable paper work. Prep counters, ovens, and other equipment will take up a lot of space, but make sure you have room for storage of your dry goods and adequate fridge and freezer space. If you're new to the bakery industry, you may want to consider hiring a designer to help you plan your kitchen.

Don't forget with all of your plans to include plenty of working space. You don't want to be climbing all over your employees when things are really busy trying to get everything out to the customer in a timely manner.

Other areas you will want to be sure to plan carefully for are:

- Delivery
- Storage
- Refrigeration and freezing
- Garbage and recycling
- Restroom
- Office
- Break area
- Customer service

Customer Service

Customer Service is an aspect of running a food business that many people assume they understand because they have experience as a consumer. We know good customer service when we see it and we know bad customer service when we experience it. Now that you are the one behind the counter, you should review your own assumptions and more importantly write down your process and policies so that your employees are as vigilant as you in creating positive customer experiences. Never more than now, in the age of internet reviews, Yelp.com, Twitter and social networking, has a commitment to superior customer service been so important to a bakery's success.

Satisfaction Guarantee

What will you do when a mistake happens? Create a policy in writing to inform your customers of your excellent satisfaction guarantee. For example, explain your policy if you make an error. For extreme errors, offer the choice of a partial refund, complimentary items or a credit for a free cupcake in the future. Of course individual circumstances require individual solutions, but it is a good idea to let customers and potential customers know you respect the adage "the customer is always right," and that you will fix any problems that arise.

Online reputation management

The key to maintaining a good reputation is a great product and great customer service. A positive demeanor, quick response to customer concerns and friendly service in all situations are critical. The way you protect your business is explicit clarity in writing on every possible customer situation that you can image and making sure your employees are well versed in these processes. If you do cupcake events/catering, make sure all of your policies are included in a contract or agreement signed by both parties. When the father of the bride calls up with buyer's remorse a week after the wedding, complaining about some "mistake" you've made, you can refer to the contract signed by a responsible party. Additionally, you should capture with a digital photograph the cupcake tower upon delivery. The documentation of a successful installation protects you from any mistakes made by employees of the reception venue. At all times be courteous, inquisitive and respectful. If you've made an honest mistake, own up to it; offer the proper remuneration and move on.

Word gets around quickly when a business owner or employee behind the counter is less than pleasant. In the same vein, word also gets around when a cupcake business has not only great products, but also friendly service. When it is a real pleasure to do business with you, your customers will return to you more frequently and refer new people to you. Whether you're a one-man or one-woman shop or have a team of employees, even more important than the quality of your product is the quality of your customer service. Customers should be greeted with smiles, welcomed like long-lost friends and catered to as much as possible. The experience they have every time they walk through the door of your business makes a difference about what kind of business you have the next year.

EXPENSES

Besides your lease and building expenses, there are several other expenses you need to anticipate. One of the biggest mistakes new business owners make is not planning wisely for the amount of capital needed, which is typically at least twice what you think it will be.

Research Costs
Research is an important component in developing your cupcake business. You've already invested in research with the purchase of this book. Basic business costs can be researched online at costhelper.com. Any books you purchase or courses you take are also part of your research costs. Keep all receipts, including automobile expenses as you will probably be driving and researching your competition, conducting traffic pattern surveys, checking out perspective locations, etc.

Working Capital
It is important to have cash on hand to run your cup-

cake business. This includes cash to buy supplies, provide change, petty cash, and any unforeseen expenses that happen all the time.

Advertising

It goes without saying that there will be costs to promote your new cupcake business. Advertising may include the costs associated with building a website, placing a Yellow Pages ad, signage, paid listings, newspaper ads, and more. Additionally, there are the costs associated with any promotions you may conduct in the first few weeks or months of your business such as discounts.

Legal Fees and Insurance

Consulting an attorney is important in starting your business. There will be costs associated with this legal advice such as setting up a legal business entity, review of your contracts, registration of your business name, etc. Adequate insurance, like liability protection, is another unexpected expense to starting a business that you can't afford to be without.

Labor

While you may not have many employees at first, you may need to hire short-term labor for any work -- renovation, sign installation, painting, electrical, plumbing, etc. -- required to get up and running.

Licenses and Permits

Licensing costs range from location to location and run from small amounts to hundreds of dollars per year. Make sure you budget these expenses.

Slush Fund

You should have enough money to run your business for several months, taking into account all of the operating expenses upfront. This is a safety net that most businesses fail to think about and ultimately is the reason they close.

When first starting, you really don't know the ebb and flow of sales and expenses. Depending on when you start your business, sales may be explosive, but then experience a natural plateau. For example, you may have big sales during the holidays then slower sales in January, then another uptick in February for Valentines Day.

Having the cash to stay afloat during slow times is the difference between success and failure. In addition to bakery equipment, you will need phone service, a dedicated phone line for processing credit cards, internet service, front end displays, a cash register, and other business equipment. Most importantly, you may have an unexpected expense such as a major repair, or an insurance deductable.

Equipment

The oven for your cupcake business can cost $10,000-$20,000. While you may be able to finance the purchase, you need to plan for the expense, as well as your additional equipment expenses. It's best to start with the least amount of equipment possible and add only what you need as you need it. Be frugal and careful. Keep all equipment maintained to prolong its life.

While many pieces of kitchen equipment can safely be purchased used, refrigeration equipment should not. Be sure to shop wisely and reserve your capital expenditures for the most important piece of equipment: your oven.

Supplies to Consider

(This will vary depending on the scale of your cupcake business.)

Baking Supplies
Greaseproof paper
Tissue paper
Foil
Icing scraper or comb
Icing ruler or comb

Serrated knife

Kitchen Equipment – Prepping, Baking & Cooking
Double stack oven(s)
Range top

EXPENSES

Countertop Mixer
Blender
Food Processor
Loader
20 quart Hobart mixer
Refrigerated display case
Double door commercial refrigerators
Microwave
Scale
Cupcake Pans
Sheet Pans
Oven Peels
Gm/Oz Scale
Saucepans
Knives
Timer
Oven Thermometer
Whisks
Thermometers
Wooden Spoons
Measuring Cups
Oven Mitts
Sieve
Dough Scrapers
Ladles
Pastry Brushes
Sifter
Measuring spoons

Beverage Supplies
Coffee Maker
Coffee Pots
Coffee Mill
Cappuccino Maker
Coffee Syrups
Juicer
Espresso Machine
Ice Machine
Water filtering system

Kitchen Equipment – Storage
Reach-in refrigerator unit (prep)
Single unit line refrigeration
Double unit line refrigeration
Walk in refrigerator and freezer
Upright freezer
Counter Freezer
Chest Freezer
Cooling Racks
Flour Bins
Baskets
Dough Tubs
Shelving

Kitchen Equipment – Cleanup

Triple sink
Garbage Disposal
Handsink
Dishwasher
Hand wash single sink
Prep sinks
Grey water sink

Dining Room
Tables
Chairs
Bar stools
Menus
Menu Board
Tablecloths
Lamps, lighting
Self-service counter for coffee prep
Bookshelf/newsrack
Music system, stereo

Office Equipment
Computer
Desk
Chair
Printer
File Cabinet
Cash Register
Register Tape
Letterhead and envelopes
Purchase orders

Receipt Pads
File Folders
Counter
Telephone
Fax

Cleaning Supplies
Garbage cans
Mop and Bucket
Mopheads
Brooms
Dustpans
Bleach
Handsoap
Floorsoap
Kitchen Soap
Garbage Bags

Miscellaneous Supplies
Dishes-plates, saucers, etc.
Glasses, coffee cups
Flatware
Paper Bags
Boxes –cupcakes to go
Plastic wrap
Aluminum foil
Paper cups
Napkins

Receiving
200 lb. receiving scale
box knife
(2) dunnage rack 36"

Storage
Dry storage
(2) #10 can racks
(4) wire shelving w/post
(4) dunnage rack 36 inch
(6) 36 gallon ingredient bin w/slidecover
(6) polycarbonate food box 18 X 26 X 15 inch

(6) polycarbonate food box 18 X 26 X 9 inch
(6) polycarbonate food box - 18 X 26 X 6 inch
(6) polycarbonate food box - 18 X 26 X 3 inch
(54) polycarbonate food box cover 18 X 26
(12) polycarbonate food box - 12 X 18 X 9 inch
(12) polycarbonate food box cover 12 X 18
(6) 12 quart round containers w/lid

Cold storage
(1) refrigerator thermometer
(4 sections) wire shelving w/post
(4) dunnage racks 36 inch
(6) polycarbonate food box - 18 X 26 X 15 inch
(24) polycarbonate food box - 18 X 26 X 9 inch
(6) drain trays for food boxes - 18 X 26 inch

(6)polycarbonate food box - 12 X 18 X 9 inch
(12) polycarbonate food box - 12 X 18 X 6 inch
(18) polycarbonate food box cover 12 X 18
(6) 12 quart round containers w/lid
(6) 8 quart round storage container w/lid
(6) 3.5 quart round storage container w/lid
(6) 2 quart round storage container w/lid
(1) 28 gallon lettuce container w/dolly

142

EXPENSES

Bake Preparation
(4 sets) measuring spoons
(1 set) dry measures
(4) 1 cup measure
(2) 24 ounce aluminum scoop
(2) 32 ounce aluminum scoop
(2) 84 ounce aluminum scoop
(1) dough scale
(1) 24 inch french whip
(2) 18 inch french whip

Utensils
13 inch serving spoons solid
13 inch serving spoons slotted
12 inch spring tongs
9.5 inch spring tongs

Bus Station/Ware Washing
(2) dishwashers aprons
(1) maximum hold thermometer
(18)   plate/tray racks
(10) flatware washing baskets
(4) all purpose racks
(2) 20 inch pot brush
(2) each 8 inch pot brush
(2) each bake pan brush
(12) each stainless metal
sponges
(12) each green pads

General Cleaning Supply
Hand and nail brushes
(2) each Hi-Lo brushes
w/squeegee
(1) each drain brush
(1) each steam kettle brush
(2) each coffee urn brushes
(1) each stack oven brush

(4) each heavy duty hand
brush
(12) each 16 ounce spray bottle
(144) each hand towels
(2) each mop buckets and
wringer
(2) each mops
(2) each wet floor signs
(1) each counter brush
(2) each floor brooms
(6) each 28 gallon grey trash
can w/lids
(3) each dollies for 28 gallon
trash can
(4) each rectangular trash cans

Buying Used Equipment

You can often save a significant amount of money by purchasing your equipment used. Just as with car buying, however, there are pros and cons to buying used. For example, you should be cautious when buying refrigeration equipment used, as repair costs can quickly add up. You may end up spending more money than if you had just bought it new.

A second down side to buying used equipment is that it will not include the warranties typically included in a new purchase. Used equipment from auctions, closed businesses and eBay/Craigslist, etc. are almost always sold "as is." Meaning, as soon as it breaks down, the cost to repair is your responsibility. The good news is that many pieces of bakery equipment are nearly indestructible. If one small part goes, you can contact the manufacturer for a replacement part. Keep in mind, this requires a bit of extra effort on your part to track down parts. Certain items such as mixers are better suited to buy used, and are known to work properly for a long time.

There are several auction sites where you can shop for used professional equipment, like eBay, and Craigslist, but you should also check local auctions and closing restaurants in the region. Auctionzip.com is the easiest way to find local auctions that often include restaurant/bakery inventory.

11

MANAGING YOUR BUSINESS

You've planned and planned and you're finally open for business. The hard work is done, right? What you will discover is that managing your business efficiently and profitably takes your time, determination, and energy every day. Many businesses fail because owners get through the planning stage and stop paying attention.

Managing Cash Flow

One of the biggest problems facing bakery owners is being able to maintain adequate cash flows. Without adequate cash, a business will not remain viable. Understanding and managing your bakery's cash flow is crucial to your success.

The Concept of Cash Flow

Cash flow is simply the movement of money in and out of your bakery. Cash comes in from the sale of your products and services and goes out for the cost of your expenses like labor, ingredients, and rent.

Prepare Your Profit and Loss Statement

Remember all the work you did to create your business plan? Part of that process was developing financial statements, including a profit and loss statement. As a start-up business, your profit and loss statement is based on estimates, but once you open your business, you can use your accounting software to create actual profit and loss statements.

You should complete your profit and loss statement before preparing your cash flow statement. Use your cash flow statement as a tool to help you control costs. Unlike other statements, this financial report helps you understand how much cash is coming in and out of your business for a given period.

The Cash Flow Statement

Especially during your first year of business, you should create a cash flow statement every month and keep tight control over where your money is going. The earlier you can recognize cash flow problems, the sooner you can address the issues, control the cash leaks, and tighten up your budget.

Cash flow is critical to the success of your business, and even if you are using an accountant or accounting service to prepare your financial documents, it is important that you understand what they're telling you. A cash flow statement is a prepared financial tool that shows you if more cash is coming in than going out, or if you are spending more than you're taking in. Cash flow statements are produced at the end of each month. It is not uncommon for start up businesses to have negative cash flow in the first months or even year of operation. The key is to have enough cash to get your business through those difficult months to profitability. Moreover, your cash flow statement will demonstrate the sources of your cash and the sustainability of your business. In other words, are you running your bakery from your cash sales or are you drawing from loans, savings or other income? Once you are able to pay your bills from your daily operation, you should begin working on the growth of your business. Accordingly, you may have a period of increased spending to accommodate greater capacity – more raw materials, advertising, salary, etc. Of course, greater capacity will hopefully yield increased revenue and the cash coming in will once again outpace the payments going out.

Sample Cash Flow Statement

Revenue

Receipts		
Cash sales		
Loans received		
Grants received		
Other income		
Capital injected		
Asset disposal		
Total Receipts	$	$

Payments

Material purchases - Cash		
Material purchases - Creditors		
Sub-contractors		
Audit / Accounting fees		
Bus dev. - travel		
Bus. dev. - entertainment		
Bus. dev. - meals		
Capital acquisitions		

Start a Cupcake Business Today

Item		
Charitable contributions		
Commissions		
Conferences and seminars		
Consulting fees		
Depreciation	n/a	n/a
Employee benefits		
Entertainment		
Equipment lease		
Facilities - insurance		
Facilities - phone		
Facilities - property taxes		
Facilities -rent		
Facilities - security		
Facilities - utilities		
Facility - other		
Financial charges		
Furniture		
Insurance		
IT consulting		
Legal fees		
Loan capital		
Loan interest		
Miscellaneous		
Office supplies		
Payroll - operational staff		
Payroll - administrative Staff		
Payroll - owner / directors		
Payroll - sales / marketing		
Payroll taxes		
Postal / Shipping		
PR / Advertising		
Repairs and maintenance		

Research and development		
Storage		
Subscriptions and dues		
Taxes and licenses		
Telecommunications		
Vehicle expenses		

Total Payments	$	$

Net Cash Flow	$	$

Opening Cash Balance	$	$
Receipts	$	$
Payments	$	$

Closing Cash Balance	$	$

Managing Employees

Managing employees effectively starts before you hire them, because before you should hire an employee you should have a clear idea of what you need from an employee. This expense is a large draw from your profits, so make sure the money is well spent.

Are you hiring someone who will eventually take over some of the management duties such as running the front counter (sales) or are you hiring someone who will take over some of the lower-end duties such as cleaning and repetitive decorating? Describing what you need in an employee should ultimately take the form of a clear and concise job description that identifies the education level and skills needed with an outline of the job duties that will be performed by the person hired. With that description in hand, you will be more effective in advertising for, interviewing, and choosing the right people to fill the positions in your bakery.

Follow these procedures when hiring employees:

[ ] Obtain a federal employment identification number by filing IRS Form SS-4.

[ ] Register with your state's employment department for payment of unemployment compensation taxes and file IRS Form 940-EZ to report your federal unemployment tax each year.

[ ] Set up a payroll system for withholding taxes and making payroll tax payments to the IRS. IRS Publication 15, Circular E, *Employer's Tax Guide*.

[ ] Get workers' compensation insurance and alert new hires of thier rights to workers' comp. benefits.

[ ] Familiarize yourself with Occupational Safety and Health Administration (OSHA) requirements and prepare an Injury and Illness Prevention Plan.

[ ] Contact the federal Department of Labor and your state labor department for information on notices you must post in the workplace.

[ ] Create an employment application for each type of position you will fill.

[ ] Create an employee handbook.

Payroll

The smartest thing you can do to make sure your payroll is handled efficiently is to outsource it. Hiring a bookkeeper or accountant to help you get set up; or purchase *Quicken Home and Business* (Intuit), *QuickBooks* (Intuit), or similar small business accounting software. You do not want to get to the end of the year and find out that you've forgotten to withhold the right amount of taxes from an employee's paycheck. If you offer benefits like health insurance and retirement, or if you have employees who receive federal earned income credit payments, this can complicate payroll even further.

The small fee charged by a local accountant or payroll firm will be well worth the cost. If you cannot afford to hire a payroll company, at the very least invest in payroll software that will calculate federal, state, and local tax withholdings. Paychex.com is a good solution for simplifying your payroll or if you're already using Quickbooks to manage your bookkeeping, consider Intuit Payroll http://payroll.intuit.com/

Business Accounting Software

Business accounting software assists you with your financial recording needs, which should be meticulously recorded. If you're starting out small and comfortable with an online solution you can begin with the free versions of Quickbooks or Outright and work your way to the paid version as your business grows.

Once you need a pro solution, you can purchase the software and hire a bookkeeper or accountant to help you get set up and explain what you need to record. Today's accounting software keeps track of transactions that in the past were required to be recorded manually in a ledger. Once the business accounting software records the information, it is capable of performing functions such as running reports, analyzing expenditures, computing cost of goods sold, and more.

Typical business accounting software packages can

download expenses directly from your credit card and bank accounts, so make sure you keep personal accounts and business transactions separate. Quickbooks can handle functions such as accounts payable, accounts receivable, profit and loss statements and payroll. It's like having a CPA living in your computer.

There is financial software available specifically designed for bakeries. BakeSmart is a bakery management software program from LegacyUSA. The software was programmed with input from experts in the industry, and offers a more customized order, inventory, production, employee management, and accounting service than you might otherwise find.

Managing Profits

In the first years of your business, your profits should be reinvested into the business as much as you can afford to do so. Do you need a company car, or do you need to advertise your wedding cupcake delivery service to hotels?

Many business owners get caught up in the idea that they need to look like they own a business, and pull profits out of the company for frivolous things. If you want your bakery to grow and thrive, you need to reinvest in it as much as possible. Living lean in the first few years can ensure that you're around for the long haul.

Managing Vendors

Building relationships with vendors is crucial. Not only will it be difficult for you to secure credit when you first open your business because of your lack of credit rating as a business, but it will take some time to understand how much you need in supplies, meaning you may be calling your vendor to place a special order when you suddenly run short.

At the same time, you should not rely solely on one

vendor to provide all that you need. What if the vendor goes out of business or suddenly raises prices? Over-reliance on a single vendor can be devastating to a small cupcake business.

Effective vendor management requires you to understand what you need to run your business, know which vendors can meet your needs, and seek the most competitive prices and service levels possible.

Vendor management is often overlooked as part of the business management process, but building relationships with your vendors that are mutually beneficial ensures that quality ingredients and supplies are available for your business when you need them.

Tips for Effective Vendor Management

Establish a Liaison. Whether it is you or another employee in your business, establish clear lines of responsibility within your business for vendor management. Your vendors should have specific contacts within your business with whom they can develop a relationship. Your vendor manager should have good negotiation and organization skills, and be able to communicate your needs clearly.

Develop Strategic Partnerships. Is there a store with whom you can develop a relationship that benefits you both? Perhaps you provide all of the baked goods for a restaurants dessert line and they supply you with coffee and referrals or advertising. Looking for ways to enhance both of your businesses converts a vendor into a partner.

Clear Communication. The best success comes when you are clear about your business needs. Work out any concerns you have before entering into any kind of long-term arrangement. Be sure the vendor will be able to grow with you.

Fair but Airtight Contracts. The details of your relationship with your vendor should be clearly spelled out in your contract. The contract should cover all the main concerns of both parties, but should be fair to both as well.

Create a Vendor Database. Having the supplies and ingredients you need keeps your customers happy, so always have backup vendors. Create a database of available vendors with notes about what they can provide for you. The last thing you want is an interruption in your ability to meet your customer's needs because you couldn't get the ingredients to make all the cupcakes on your menu.

Managing Expenses

Gross Profit Margin is the difference between the sales you generate in your cupcake business and the cost paid out to create your product. Here is a simple example: If it costs you $0.80 to make a cupcake and you sell it for $2.50, your **gross profit** is $1.70 and your **gross profit margin** is 68%. Keep in mind that you must calculate all of your sales and expenses related to producing your cupcakes when creating this ratio. Your gross profit margin is a good indication of the health of your business revealing the proportion of money left over from revenues to pay fixed expenses and for future savings. A gross profit margin is also a concrete number you will be able to use to establish credit, obtain loans, and grow your business. One of the best ways to improve your gross profit margin is by managing your expenses. Selling more cupcakes does not necessarily mean more profit if your expenses are too high. Moreover, you have much more control over how much you spend than over who chooses to buy from you.

By reducing your expenses, you can lower your break-even point, which means it becomes easier to make a profit. There are many things you can do to control expenses:

- Negotiate better prices with vendors
- Don't make more cupcakes or store more inventory than you need
- Make sure your prices are high enough to make a

profit without chasing customers away
- Choose a few high profit margin items to sell, like coffee.
- Analyze your cash flow and address leaks. For example: utility bills could be lowered with motion detectors, energy-saving compact fluorescent lightbulbs; eliminate expensive ingredients that don't yield a superior product.

Have you ever wondered why some cupcake shops or small food producers close for the day as soon as they sell out? At first glance it seems like they should stay open later and make more cupcakes, right? Obviously there is a greater demand than supply if they are selling out. However, this business practice protects the owner and their **gross profit margin**. Based on their food costing and analysis they know they are profitable if they sell out. Their labor and utility costs are capped. But, if they fire up the ovens again, using additional resources and paying for additional utilities and labor, they run the risk of creating waste and lowering their profit margin.

It is much better for a business to track their cupcake sales over time to see if adding additional staff will increase efficiency and output that will result in higher profit, not just higher sales.

Another idea is creating a sense of demand by producing smaller quantities of lower profit, high demand products, then upselling the higher profit comparable product. For example, many shops offer mini cupcakes and sell them for about a dollar less than full-size cupcakes (e.g. mini cupcakes sell for $1.00, full-size for $2.50). The mini cupcakes are less profitable because they are just as much labor and use almost the same amount of raw material to produce. However, consumers love them. They are bite-sized, customers try multiple flavors and they feel like they're indulging without the guilt of over-eating. The trick is to make a quantity that will sell out by the middle of the day. Customers learn to arrive early to purchase mini cupcakes, yet often purchase full-sized cupcakes to complement their order. Customers who arrive later in the day have less choice, but almost never leave empty-handed. At this point in the day, the high profit cupcake is sold, contributing to the gross profit margin.

12

MENU PLANNING

One of the most creative parts of being a cupcake business owner is determining what kind of menu you will have. Obviously, if you're famous for a certain cupcake recipe with your family and friends, it will probably be featured in your new business. However, menu planning is more than deciding upon products you want to sell. It is also about formulating and finalizing recipes, figuring food costs, and using your menu to inform the equipment selection. If you want to stay in business, you need to concentrate on planning a menu that allows you to earn enough profit to pay you plus all your monthly bills.

You do not want to purchase expensive equipment that gets little use in your menu or spend too little on the equipment you will need extensively. Many novice bakery owners save a few dollars on critical equipment such as mixers, ovens, and refrigeration only to find out that repair costs or inefficiency actually costs them far more in lost revenue. Again, early menu planning will help you think through your recipes, the time to make batches and the quantity you need to make (and sell) each day; therefore, your equipment must be able to support that quantity. Use the Cost of Goods process as discussed in Chapter 3 to help you determine the actual cost of each recipe. You know by now that the cupcake market is extremely competitive. Your menu is a huge part of determining your particular concept and will help you to differentiate yourself from other cupcake businesses.

Recipe Costing and Pricing

To determine the cost of your cupcakes so that you can set prices that will earn you profit, you need to start with the cost of the ingredients. Calculate the cost of the raw ingredients on a per-cupcake basis by taking the whole cost of the bulk ingredient and dividing by the number of cupcakes each ingredient can produce. Add together all of the ingredients in each recipe by its per-cupcake cost. Multiply the cost per cupcake by the number you expect to sell on average (for a specified period of time like a week or a month). Repeat for each cupcake recipe you sell until you have a total estimated cost.

In addition to the costs of the products themselves, you have to include all of the other costs of your business. Add up all of your costs: lease, insurance, advertising, utilities, your website, delivery costs, and anything else you have to pay for. To determine your profit, multiply the price per item sold by the number sold and subtract these additional costs. You need to adjust your prices until you are covering costs plus earning a profit.

Product Mix

There are so many recipes for a cupcake business that it can be difficult to know where to place your focus. Just a small list of available choices includes:

- Classic flavors (chocolate, vanilla, red-velvet)
- Gourmet flavors

- Wedding cupcakes
- Cupcakes in a jar
- Breakfast cupcakes
- Kids cupcakes
- Filled cupcakes
- Mini cupcakes
- Fondant covered cupcakes

As fun as the menu planning can be, determining your product mix is hard work that will require fine-tuning as you go. Part of what will determine your product mix is going back to the business plan and taking a close look at your target market and your competition. Remember, with your menu, you project a very specific kind of environment. While your menu is critical to creating the concept, the most important determinant of your product mix has to be profitability.

Yes, your *swiss meringue buttercream with bourbon-madagascar vanilla* is to die for, but it is labor intensive and at $2.50/serving, you might have to sell 500 of them to break even or make a profit, especially if it's costing you $1.25 to make each one. It is important when planning your menu that you consider having some staple items that are less labor intensive and have a high profit margin. Your goal should be to balance your offering of profitable items with popular items. Depending on your concept, you should consider targeting at least 20% of your revenue to be from beverages, because they have very low labor cost, and maintain a strong profit margin.

Creating Room for Profit

You need to think about what you can make and sell that gives you good margins. You also need to consider what kind of customers your location will attract, because if you're trying to sell $4 filled cupcakes to stay-at-home moms on a frugal budget, you might not make it. This was the mistake made by a popular Westcoast cupcake bakery. While the quality of the products were sensational, everything was high-end, low margin, and time-consuming to make. The business closed because the owner did not understand cash flow and food costing and there wasn't enough of a mix of cupcake options.

Another way to help ensure that you keep the costs of production low and make it easier to make a profit on the items you sell is to learn how to develop commercial size recipes. You may have a great recipe for oatmeal cookies, but to make it work for your business, you need to know how to make it into a commercial batch. A great book to keep handy is *Professional Baking, College Version with CD-Rom, 4th Edition by Wayne Gisslen*.

Finally, another way to help make profits easier is to streamline your production process. Most major restaurants understand the idea of streamlining; it is why they have prep cooks. The prep cooks are paid less than the chef, do most of the time-consuming work, and make it easy for meals to be prepared quickly during the peak times. The same concept can be applied to your cupcake bakery.

Other Menu Planning Considerations

If you are still in the early stages of your bakery and haven't nailed down your concept, review the following questions to aid your thought process:

- What kind of customer are you trying to attract?
- What kind of businesses are you trying to emulate?
- What will your customers most likely be doing when they stop by your cupcake shop? Will they swing in for a dozen cupcakes on the way to the office, or will they line up for the post lunch sugar fix?

- Will you cater events and/or take special orders for weddings and other parties, or are you only a take-out shop? Will you have space for "dine-in" customers, and if so, will you be serving drinks? Can your budget accommodate the extra expense of a full-service operation?

Once you know what kind of customers you will be serving and what kind of product mix you will have, you need to think about what you want to sell beyond cupcakes. One standard offering will probably be coffee, but coffee in itself opens up an entire line of questioning:

- Are you going to serve just coffee, or specialty coffees, cappuccinos, and lattes as well?
- Will you be partnering with a particular vendor and featuring a coffee brand, or just offering whatever fits your budget?
- Will you be offering soft drinks and juices as well, or simply have a fridge with a few bottled choices?

In addition to thinking about what you will serve, you need to think about presentation.

- When people order cupcakes from you, how will it be packaged, paper boxes; clear, food-safe plastic, napkins? Will everything go in boxes, or will your packaging be part of how you differentiate yourself?
- When people choose to eat their cupcake or drink a beverage in your space, will you have glass plates and cups available, or will they simply make use of the tables but have your carry out packaging? Will you need staff to clean an eat-in space and wash tables, dishes, a public restroom, etc.

161

One thing to remember when planning your menu is that you cannot be everything to everyone. Choose your angle and your approach. While you may add products and services as you grow your business, have a definitive place to start, and then practice doing what you do well.

You will never be able to please everyone who walks through your door, so don't even try. You'll quickly go out of business trying to keep enough supplies on hand to meet the tastes of everyone. Instead, have a clear vision of what type of cupcake shop you are and then perfect it.

13

AVOIDING MISTAKES

Becoming a successful business owner takes hard work and commitment. It's easy to dream about owning your own business, but the reality is that you'll end up working longer hours than when you worked for someone else, and it will be harder to leave work at the office. Yes, you will be your own boss, and you can control the direction your company takes, but you're also at the mercy of the economy, the law, and the whims of customers.

The bakery industry is physically demanding. Not only are you on your feet all day, but you're not buying five-pound bags of flour from the grocery store but 50-pound and 100-pound bulk containers of ingredients. Heavy lifting, long hours of standing, and working late into the night to prepare for the breakfast crowd is common. In addition, the work tends to be repetitious—you're often making the same things over and over again, trying to achieve a uniform look in shape, size, and design.

There are many pitfalls and challenges you will face on your way to becoming a successful business owner, and there is no way to prepare you for every scenario you might face. You might be able to avoid financial or emotional distress by considering these typical mistakes and making plans now to avoid them.

Be a Business Owner, Not a Slave to Your Business

Just because you like to bake and create delicious treats doesn't make you a good business owner. You need business sense more than you need baking sense to survive. You have to be able to wear several hats, from baker to boss, from chief bottle washer to menu planner. Make sure you don't get so wrapped up in the creative side of things that you forget to run a tight business with accurate records, paid bills, and attention to safety.

Be willing to surround yourself with legal and accounting professionals who can help you understand the financial and legal aspects of the business, and remember that if you can't turn a profit by being capable of managing expenses and making smart business decisions, you will not survive.

Don't succumb to the pressure that sometimes comes with being a new business owner of giving everything away. Your friends, if they are excited about your new business, should pay for the donut and coffee when they come in; the customer should not get a free bagel just because you don't have the flavor of donut they prefer.

Don't be afraid to seek advice from experienced business owners, either in your retail area or through online forums.

Manage Costs

One of the ways new business owners fail is by getting spend-happy in the first few months, trying to buy everything they might possible need for the business. Only buy what you need, and be tough and disciplined with your costs. Some of the major costs you will want to manage carefully and control well are labor costs, supply costs, and marketing.

Develop a budget so that you can understand where your money is going and how much you need to make to break even and make a profit. You need to have a good understanding of your costs as well as the ability to forecast your income. Costs to consider:

- Cost of goods
- Salaries/Wages/Contract labor
- Rent/mortgage
- Utilities
- Loan payments/Contract payments
- Lease payments
- Insurance premiums
- Advertising
- Transportation
- Office supplies
- All other expenses

There is a sample budget worksheet in the appendix to get you started. Be sure to adjust the worksheet to account for additional costs your business might have.

Be Flexible

To be successful, you need to be flexible. You need to be willing to work long hours, take risks, and understand that opening a business is a huge undertaking. It's easy to underestimate how much it will cost and overestimate how quickly you will become profitable.

Plan on obtaining 40-50% more capital than you think you'll need, because you probably will need it. You will not only be contending with the development of your own business but also with the unpredictability of the market, your competition, and the economy.

Commit for the Long-Term

Make sure you are ready to commit to the business for the long haul. It will take 12-18 months for the business to take off and for you to find your groove as a business owner. Be patient and tenacious. As a business owner, your number one goal is to establish and build your business.

Don't Try To Do It All Yourself

You may need at least one employee to run the counter while you're doing the baking, or you won't make enough money to survive. All it takes is burning $100 in products because you're selling a $2 cup of coffee to make you realize how incredibly important a second person can be.

Hire and Manage Employees Well

Good employees are hard to find and the bakery business, like other areas of retail, has a higher level of turnover. When choosing employees, be sure you refrain from asking anything illegal (you can't ask if someone is married or planning to have kids and whether or not that would impact their availability, for example, and you can't ask what religion the person is). A complete checklist for interviewing potential employees is in the appendix.

As a business owner, you want to find employees who will represent your business well. This is less about whether or not they have piercings and more about whether or not they come to work clean, dressed appropriately, and can smile readily and make your customers feel welcome. There are some aspects of customer service that simply cannot be trained. When you're getting ready to hire your staff, there are certain things you should keep in mind during the interview and due diligence process.

Past History. No matter how nice the person seems during the interview, you should call references and previous employers to verify the information provided and learn what you can about the person's previous employment. Former employers will often rave about good ex-employees and say nothing about bad ones. Listen to that silence.

Presentability. It may seem like common sense, but if your prospective employee doesn't care enough to dress professionally for the interview, how can you trust that he or she will care about the customer?

Personality. When choosing an employee, how you get along with the person and how you think that person will get along with your customers is important. Friendliness, self-confidence, enthusiasm, and honesty are critically important, particular for your front counter help.

Minimum Staff Needed

Depending on the size of your establishment and the amount of business you do, you may be able to get away with just one assistant or you may need a full staff. For the standard cupcake bakery, the typical number of employees may include a baker, a dishwasher, a decorator, and a counter person. Don't over-hire, but don't sell the business short, either. You need people to help you run the business.

Policies and Procedures

One of the most important things you can do for your business, both for while you are running it and when you're ready to exit the business, is to have well written, clear and concise policies and procedures. Not only should each position have clear responsibilities, but the shop as a whole should operate under a set of policies that make your expectations about harassment, food safety, and performance crystal clear.

You should also determine what benefits you will offer

and prepare a benefits manual that clearly states when an employee is eligible and what kinds of benefits are available.

Take care of your equipment

Preventative maintenance of your equipment can save you hundreds to thousands of dollars in repair bills. These unexpected repairs can be the difference between a profitable month and an unprofitable one. Being conscientious about your gear can be as easy as regularly cleaning your equipment. Also, don't put off scheduled maintenance on critical equipment such as refrigeration, ovens and mixing equipment. These are the lifeblood of any cupcake business and you can't afford to have them break down during critical times of the year. Below are a few additional suggestions for maintaining your cupcake equipment.

1.   Clean your gear every day to prevent dirt build up. This build up comes from batter, frosting and other food material falling into the crevasses. It will wear down motors, vents, and fans, thereby reducing the lifespan of your equipment.

2.   Keep a schedule for cleaning, calibrating commercial ovens, checking commercial refrigerator temperatures, and descaling dishwashers. Hobart mixers require professional servicing to maintain the correct weight of grease and oil in very specific spots. Have it checked by an authorized provider according to the maintenance schedule.

3.   Closely read and follow the cleaning directions in the manual and on the solvent bottles to avoid damaging your equipment.

4.   Contact the manufacturer if you aren't certain of the proper way to clean any bakery equipment you have. Most manufacturers keep copies of maintenance manuals even for retired models.

168

5. Set up a service contract for your restaurant equipment with the manufacturer or a local service company to perform regularly scheduled fine tuning of each piece.

6. When choosing new equipment, opt for ones that are easy to clean. This means coming apart and being put together easily.

7. Take advantage of your manufacturer's representatives. They are well trained and don't charge to help out, so call them in to teach you the best cleaning methods for your equipment.

14

GROWING YOUR BUSINESS

You should be continually striving for excellence in everything you do. As you get through those first difficult months and begin to catch your stride, you should be thinking ahead to what you envision your business being in a year, five years, even ten years.

You may be happy being just a single bakery serving a small community of loyal customers, but you may envision growth that encompasses developing an online bakery, a franchised operation, or multiple outlets.

Whatever your direction, most business owners want to grow their business and keep it thriving. There are definitely things you can do as a business owner to help ensure the ongoing success of your business.

Ultimately, even if you decide to get out of the bakery business down the road, you should keep growing your business so that it is easier to sell when you are ready to exit or retire.

Reputation

It's very easy to tarnish a good reputation but almost impossible to repair a bad one. The old adage that an unhappy customer tells ten people and a happy customer tells one is close to the truth. Strive to make the experience your customers have in your establishment the best possible. This means addressing everything from cleanliness to food quality to the service your customers receive from you and your employees.

Word-of-mouth advertising is still the most powerful advertising you can get...especially since word of mouth typically means a post on Facebook or a review on a website that hundreds or more people end up reading. Make customer service training a part of every new hire's training, and think of your role as host or hostess to be as important as every other role you play as a small business owner.

Give Back To Your Community

One of the best ways you can become a true member of your community is to become involved. Sponsor teams, spend some good will money for local sports and performance program advertising, and be a member of your Chamber of Commerce.

More than that, show pride in your community by maintaining the exterior of your business and being the type of location that enhances the area, not detracts from it. Make people feel welcome when they visit from out of town and don't be a greedy profiteer who forgets the human side of business.

Top 5 Ways to Grow Your Business

Being successful in business is hard work, but there are things you can do that will make growing your business a little bit easier.

1. Market Penetration

When most people think about business growth, they

think about ways to attract new customers and extend their reach to new markets, but the first thing you should consider is how to get more and do more for your existing customer base. Deeper market penetration is much easier to accomplish than actually expanding your market, because you already have these customers in front of you, ready to tell you what they need.

Elicit feedback from your customers about what they wish you offered but don't. Make sure your existing customers know about all the different services you offer. Just because Mr. Smith only stops in for coffee and a donut every morning doesn't mean he wouldn't turn to you for a wedding cake when his daughter gets married, so make sure your customers know everything you are capable of doing. Other ways to increase your penetration:

- Upsell and cross-sell complementary products to your customers. If they like your famous filled cupcakes, remind them that they can custom order a dozen of them when the family is in town for graduation. If someone orders coffee, offer a freshly baked cupcake to go with it. If the wedding party contracts you to do a cupcake tower, offer to do a bridal shower as well.
- Reward regular customers. Offer punch cards or discount coupons to customers who make a purchase. Offer a free cup of coffee with every dozen cupcake purchased, or send the customer home with 10% off the next purchase every time they buy.
- Reach out to the places your customers work. Offer to provide cupcakes for their next lunch meeting.

2. Referrals and Word of Mouth

Enough emphasis cannot be placed on how important customer service is, but the best way to grow your business is to make your existing customers happy so that they will go out and talk to other people about how great you are. People are more likely to buy when someone they know says it's worth it.

- If you do any specialty services like catering or wedding cupcake towers, ask your satisfied customers and clients to refer you to others who might need your services. Offer them a 10% discount for bringing in a referral card or mentioning the person who referred them. Entice new customers by getting your existing customers in on your marketing.

- Get together with other local, non-competing businesses and put together a welcome package full of coupons that realtors can give new homeowners to introduce them.

3. Extend Your Reach

Do you have the ability to deliver locally? Would your cupcakes sell well on a restaurant menu?

- There are many ways you can work to extend the reach of your business. If you build from what you already do well, it can be an easy process to adapt it to a new environment. Online cupcake shops are a viable thanks to super-fast shipping capabilities and refrigerated shipping materials. You can ship your cupcakes just about anywhere. (watch for intrastate and international restrictions on food shipments).
- Add a shopping cart function to your website that allows people (locally and not) to place orders with you. Be sure to calculate shipping accurately and to make sure you only offer items that can truly survive the shipping and transit time.
- Adding a delivery service is another great way to extend your reach, but be sure to adjust your prices overall or add a delivery fee to the total because no matter where you live, gas is an expensive addition to your cash outflow. Make sure, through market

research, that there would be enough interest in offering delivery before actually doing it.

- Partner with a local restaurant to provide your famous chocolate cupcakes for their dinner menu. Not only will they purchase the cupcakes from you, but you can often negotiate advertising as part of the deal, with your bakery's name appearing on the menu.

4. Trade Shows and Industry Networking

Attending trade shows is one of the best ways to keep up on the latest trends in the food industry, make contacts with important vendors, showcase your products, and gain new clients.

You do not want to spend all of your time at trade shows and neglect your business, but attending a couple of shows each year is smart business. Choose the shows you attend wisely and make sure they are the best ones for your particular business or niche. Stay up-to-date with the baking industry at large by being associated with an organization like the American Institute of Baking.

5. Differentiate Your Offerings

Draw new clientele by catering to specific niches like gluten-free or locally sourced ingredients. Cupcake trends are still emerging and changing, but it's a safe bet that small tasty indulgences will continue to be popular among a wide audience. Most importantly, do what you love to do!

APPENDIX

Business Plan (example)
Extreme Cupcakes, Burlington VT

APPENDIX

1.0 Executive Summary

The Concept

Thanks primarily to Starbucks, within the past 20 years the coffeehouse has become a familiar feature of American life and luxury has gone mainstream. Every day, millions of Americans stop for an espresso-based coffee drink. People who would not have dreamed of spending more than $0.50 for a cup of coffee a few years ago now gladly pay $3 to $5 for their cappuccino, mocha latte or vanilla ice blended drink.

The specialty-coffee business is growing at a healthy pace. During the past 20 years, there has not been a single year, despite war and recession, in which specialty coffee sales have not grown. In many years the increase has been in double digits. In addition, no coffeehouse chains have failed during this time, although the list of casualties in other industries is quite long.

Starbucks and other chains serve average quality pastries in establishments that have the same generic design appearance. Indeed, there is a need for specialty cupcakes as well to accompany the specialty coffee in the market. A lot of major restaurant chains and food purveyors are adding chef inspired dishes to their menus, providing an opportunity for *Extreme Cupcakes* to capture the chef inspired cupcake category that is emerging in larger metropolitan areas including LA and New York.

A niche exists that has yet to be filled for a high-volume, upscale, quality-driven cupcake coffeehouse with a hip, inviting atmosphere. Extreme Cupcakes will make the best cupcakes in the country. We will offer high-quality products in an upscale environment. Furthermore, the marketplace district in Burlington, VT provides a mixed customer base of *University of Vermont* students and local businesspeople that will maintain high levels of business in every season, at all times of the day, every day of the week.

Extreme Cupcakes will provide a hip, comfortable atmosphere where the customer can receive quality food, service and entertainment at a reasonable price. The coffeehouse will offer a variety of choices to the customers. Coffee and tea of all sorts will be offered. Juice, soda, and non-alcoholic beverages will also be available. Cupcakes will be made for wholesale as well as retail and there will be a cupcake delivery person for the local businesses in a five block radius.

At night the setting will change to a lounge, which will attract customers going to nightclubs. In the evening, both wine and beer will be on sale. There will be nightly entertainment featuring rhythm and blues and jazz. On selected nights there will be poetry readings, karaoke and an open microphone. The walls will be used as an art gallery and from time to time there will be an artist in residence.

Start a Cupcake Business Today

The site contains an 800 square foot building which was used as a restaurant. Remodeling will consist of removing the existing booths, adding a coffee bar and some new furniture. The kitchen will need some remodeling to convert it into a bakeshop. The property is currently zoned for restaurants.

The interior design of the building will focus on a contemporary modern style with a young hip hop lounge feel. Extreme will have a long coffee bar with a pastry cases full of cupcakes.

Founder

The owner, Paula Spencer has been in the baking industry all her life. She received training from all the major baking institutions in the country. She has also worked in every aspect of the food industry. See attached resume.

Financials

The company anticipates rapid acceptance of the Extreme Cupcakes concept in Burlington, VT with revenues of $462,000 in the first fiscal year, rising to more than $520,000 in FY 2010. Net profit is projected to be approximately $56,519 in 2009, growing to an estimated $78,881 by 2010.

Highlights

An advanced and expandable point-of-sale system

After carefully tracking the performance of the store through an expandable and highly detailed point-of-sale system, we will use this as a "blueprint" for expansion. For example, daily sales are tracked and analyzed by item, time period and cost of goods. Labor requirements are matched to projected in-store sales based upon past performance for maximum efficiency. Even after paying higher than average wages, we expect to allocate no more than 25% to labor costs and no more than 33% on food cost. Our key economic driver will be a *profit per employee* denominator.

1.1 Mission Statement

To make the best cupcakes in the country in a high-volume, upscale, quality-driven cupcake coffeehouse with a hip, inviting atmosphere.

1.2 Keys to Success

Keys to success for Extreme Cupcakes will include:

APPENDIX

- Providing the highest quality product (best cupcake in the country)

- Combing the high demand for fast quality coffee and pastry on-the-go with delivery service for those with no time to wait in line

- A relaxing, upscale interior design

- Prime site selection with an upscale affluent population, year-round tourist activity, heavy pedestrian traffic by the site, a dynamic student population and a heavy concentration of local businesses

- A market that exposes Extreme to high-profile "trend-setters" and "key influencers"

- Ongoing, aggressive marketing

- Highly trained and friendly staff

- Multiple revenue streams including gift baskets, coffee gift/frequency cards and wholesale accounts with local grocery stores, gas stations and other food service establishments

- A dynamic website with online sales capability

- Very extensive wholesale accounts of hotels, supermarkets and gas stations

1.3 Risks
- Will there be a demand as we believe for upscale cupcakes?
- Will the health fad overwhelm the gourmet fad?
- Will the business be able to stay afloat when school is out?

2.0 Company Summary

Extreme Cupcakes launches with its first cupcake/coffeehouse located in downtown Burlington. Extreme will offer residents and visitors a totally new style of cupcake shop - one offering an assortment of gourmet cupcakes, uniquely flavorful coffee drinks and a comfortable, upscale environment at which to socialize, relax or work.

- **Variety:** No other cupcake/coffeehouse in the area will provide the range of cupcakes, coffee drinks, tea, hot chocolate,

179

juice, smoothies and other products that Extreme does.

- **Location:** Extreme Cupcakes will be located in the prime section of downtown Burlington in the heart of the downtown shopping district. Extreme locations are designed for high volume year round, with revenues and profits to match.

- **Expansion:** Assuming this store is successful, it will be the first of a chain of Extreme Cupcakes coffeehouses located in markets that have similar demographic profiles, significant traffic by the store, year-round tourist activity and a sizeable student population.

At one time Pizza Hut and Domino's were the only quality pizza chains in America. Then came Papa John's. And then California Pizza Kitchen, with its superb product and quality. Extreme will be the first "Lexus" of the cupcake/coffeehouse chain industry, offering a higher quality product and better quality service in an exceptional environment like California Pizza Kitchen. It will be like a fusion of all the best attributes of Starbucks with a hip young twist. There will be no cupcake/coffeehouse that will come close to being as upscale as our concept.

2.1 Company Ownership
Extreme Cupcakes is a privately held corporation. It is registered as a state Subchapter S Corporation in the State of Vermont with ownership by Paula Spencer and other outside investors.

2.2 Start-up Summary
Start-up expenses are still to be determined once there is an inspection of the space available.

3.0 Products

Cupcakes
We will produce assortment of Cupcakes

Filled Collection:

Chocolate: chocolate cupcake filled with vanilla buttercream, frosted with chocolate glaze and chocolate buttercream

APPENDIX

Vanilla: Vanilla cupcake filled with vanilla buttercream, frosted with vanilla bean glaze and buttercream

Orange: vanilla cupcake filled with orange buttercream and frosted with orange buttercream and with an orange glaze topping

Lemon Meringue: Lemon curd filled and swiss meringue frosting on a vanilla cupcake.

Fruit Collection: A vanilla cupcake filled with fruit filling and dusted with powdered sugar and a small crest of corresponding buttercream frosting

Raspberry: Raspberry preserve filling; Raspberry buttercream

Strawberry: Strawberry preserve filling; Strawberry buttercream

Lemon: Lemon curd filling; Vanilla buttercream

The King Collection: Traditional Cupcakes with contemporary twist

Banana Nut: Banana cupcake frosted with chocolate buttercream and topped with pecans or walnuts

Black Forest: Chocolate cupcake topped with chocolate ganache and brandied cherries

Red Velvet: All-natural chocolate red velvet cupcake with cream cheese frosting

German Chocolate- Chocolate cupcake with coconut pecan caramel frosting

The Unexpected Collection: Various versions of fruit flavors

Pineapple Inside Out Cupcake- Vanilla cupcake topped with buttercream and caramelized pineapple

Caramel Apple- Vanilla cupcake topped with buttercream and caramelized apple

The Pie Collection- Various pies converted into cupcake versions

Apple pie: Vanilla cupcake with apple topping and cinnamon frosting sprinkled with cinnamon sugar

Key Lime: Vanilla with lime cupcake, creamcheese frosting with crushed graham crackers mixed into a cream filling.

Chocolate Silk: Chocolate cupcake, chocolate filling, Dusted with half powdered sugar and half cocoa with buttercream top

Pecan: Chocolate cupcake with chopped pecans in the batter, topped with buttercream

The New Collection:

Mocha- Chocolate cupcake with coffee essence in chocolate buttercream
Golden Cupcake- Vanilla cupcake; vanilla buttercream frosting with vanilla bean and gold sprinkles on top
PB Cup- Chocolate Cupcake with peanut buttercream filling with milk chocolate frosting

DRINKS

Espresso Drinks

Espresso: A double shot of straight espresso
Café Americano: Espresso combined with hot water, a gourmet brewed coffee
Cappuccino: Espresso with a smooth topping of milk foam
Café Latte: Espresso combined with steamed milk, topped with a small amount of velvety milk foam
Café Mocha: A Café Latte combined with Ghirardelli chocolate, topped with whipped cream and chocolate shavings
Espresso Macchiato: A straight shot of espresso topped with a spoonful of rich milk foam
Espresso Con Panna: A straight shot of espresso topped with a generous dollop of whipped cream
"Morning Buzz": Espresso combined with our gourmet coffee of the day to get your day going.

Coffee

The Banana Nut Cafe: Coffee. Warm milk. Banana, macadamia nut and vanilla syrups. Topped with whipped cream and cinnamon dusting

The Cafe Amaretto Coffee. Warm milk. Amaretto and vanilla syrups topped with whipped cream and almonds

Flavored Espresso

Vanilla Cappuccino: Cappuccino made with vanilla flavored milk foam

Vanilla Latte: A Caffe Latte with vanilla essence added

White Chocolate Latte: Espresso, white chocolate flavoring and steamed milk topped with velvety foam and white chocolate shavings

The 50/50 Latte: Espresso. Vanilla and orange syrups, steamed milk and whipped cream topping

The Raspberry Mocha Latte Coffee. Raspberry and chocolate syrups. Half and half. Whipped cream topping

Chai Latte: Espresso. Chai. Steamed milk and whipped cream

Hot Chocolate

French Vanilla: Hot chocolate with vanilla and whipped cream.
White Chocolate: Hot chocolate with white chocolate and whipped cream
Chocolate Truffle: Rich dark hot chocolate with whipped cream topping
Holiday Spice: Rich hot chocolate and holiday spices. Topped with whipped cream

Peppermint: Rich chocolate and refreshing peppermint. Topped with whipped cream

Smoothies

The Espresso Chocolate Malt: Chocolate malt for grownups
The Double Dutch Chocolate Smoothie: The Mocha Smoothie
The Vanilla Smoothie: Rich natural vanilla flavor
50/50 Smoothie (Orange and Vanilla) A 50's favorite

Iced Teas

The Classic
A southern sweet tea.
The Arnold Palmer
Half tea and half lemonade.
Mint
Sweet tea with mint and lemon.
Jasmine
Jasmine sweet tea

Hot Tea

Earl Grey
English Breakfast
Peppermint
Herb Apricot
Earl Grey
Lavender
Darjeeling
Formosa Oolong
Golden Flowers Herbal
Herbal Lemon

Juices
Fresh squeezed orange juice
Old-fashioned Lemonade
Strawberry Juice
Apple Juice (regular and sparkling)

Other

Milk
Soymilk
Bottled Water

4.0 Market Analysis
Extreme Cupcakes' focus is on meeting the demand of a regular local resident, students and downtown workers as a customer base, as well as a significant level of tourist traffic from nearby hotels.

4.1 Market Segmentation
Extreme focuses on the middle- and upper-income markets. These market segments consume the majority of coffee and espresso prod-

ucts. Burlington in the mid-1990s had only a handful of specialty coffee retailers: San Francisco Roasters, Cafe Diem, Cafe Intermezzo, Aurora Coffee, J. Martinez, and others. Now, coffee roasters, shops, and suppliers take more than two full pages in the Yellow Pages. Burlington is currently in the middle of a building and population explosion. Young singles and couples are choosing to reject long commutes in favor of living closer to their work and recreational venues. With the extra time that comes from being in a vibrant growing city with an active nightlife, neighborhoods that were formerly dotted with a limited number of night spots have seen their neighborhoods burgeon with new venues.

Local Customers

Extreme wants to establish a large regular customer base of students and local business people. This will establish a healthy, consistent revenue base to ensure stability of the business. To reach locals we will offer special discount cards, pass out free coffee coupons at events and offer entertainment on weekends.

Tourists

Tourist traffic comprises approximately 15% of the revenues.

Relationship with concierges, great reviews, heavy promotion and competitive products and service are critical to capture this segment of the market.

Wholesale accounts

Wholesale accounts should build slowly and hopefully will account for over 30% of revenues. To help supplement the times when school is out and businesses are off. We will establish relationship with local hotels, grocery stores and gas stations.

4.1.1 Market Analysis

The chart and table below outline the total market potential of the above-described customer segments.

Market Analysis						
		2007	2008	2009	2010	
Potential Customers	Growth					CAGR
Local Residents	10%	100,725	110,798	121,878	134,066	10.00%
Tourists/Visitors	15%	36,915	42,452	48,820	56,143	15.00%
Downtown Workers	20%	28,020	33,624	40,349	48,419	20.00%
Total	12.87%	165,660	186,874	211,047	238,628	12.87%

4.2 Target Market Segment Strategy

The dominant target market for Extreme Cupcakes is a regular stream of local residents. Personal and expedient customer service and a friendly atmosphere with cupcakes sold at a competitive price is the key to maintaining the local market share of this target market. The immediate market area of Extreme Cupcakes includes the communities of Downtown, South Burlington, Williston, Shelburne, Charlotte, East Burlington, Winooski, Park Hills, and adjacent towns. The market segment is largely made up of singles between the ages of 20 and 40, married couples in the same age bracket without children, graduate and professional students attending area universities, tourists, and conventioneers.

4.2.1 Market Needs

According to the *Encyclopedia of Emerging Industries*, 3rd ed "Whether it was the "Hard Rock Cafe" or "Planet Hollywood" or one small "Nouvelle Cuisine" restaurant that opened in the heart of Ohio's Amish country, all over the United States creative dining became the rule for any eatery. Barbecued pulled pork was once considered a unique taste treat in uptown Manhattan. Sushi and Creole cooking often were considered exotic in Middle America. The next millionaire, or billionaire, in the food market was the person or company who could come up with yet one more interesting concept to excite diners of all ages, ethnic groups, and tastes." Another emerging concept in the early twenty-first century is the "fast-casual" restaurant, which like fast-food chains does not have a dining room wait staff, and therefore, no tipping. However, the fast-casual restaurant offers a higher-quality menu than the fast-food chains.

Luxurious items are in demand for the common person so Extreme cupcake will be the equivalent of Starbuck espresso 10 years ago. Because Burlington has a cool climate for the summer and cold climate for the winter, coffee and tea products are very much in demand all year long along. Much of the day's activity occurs in the morning hours before ten a.m., with a relatively steady flow for the remainder of the day.

4.3 Service Business Analysis
The retail coffee industry in the U.S. has recently experienced rapid growth. Coffee drinkers in the Burlington are finicky about the quality of beverages offered at the numerous coffee bars across the region. Despite low competition in the immediate area, Extreme will position itself as a place where customers can enjoy a delicious fresh pastry with a cup of delicious coffee in a relaxing environment.

4.3.1 Competition and Buying Patterns
Competition in the Burlington for artisan cupcakes is not present and nobody provide nearly the level of product quality and customer service as Extreme Cupcakes. Local customers are looking for a high quality product in a relaxing atmosphere. They desire a unique, upscale experience. *Specialty Coffee Retailers Association* believes the market has not approached maturity and, as yet, no coffee chain has differentiated itself significantly from the others. Customer guest check averages are rising. As pastries, chocolates, tea, pre-packaged sandwiches, snacks, juice drinks and gift items are added to the menu, the average customer expenditure has risen. Extreme expects that guest checks will average in the $4 - $6 range. We will do about 60% cupcakes and 30% beverages from walk in customers.

In June 2005, food research and consulting firm Technomic released its Top 500 Chain Restaurant Annual Report. According to Technomic, bakery items as a category continued to be a growth leader in 2004, with sales increasing 9.2% over the prior year exceeding the restaurant industry average of 7.2% growth in 2004. (Although this was down more than 50% from 2003, where the pastry category led all segments.) The related bakery café segment grew at 22% in 2004, providing more evidence that Americans still like their carbohydrates. Industry observers agree that cupcakes represent fun, a treat and a personal indulgence that will continue to outweigh concerns about health and expanding waistlines for many tears to come.

Sales of large pies, snack pies, full- size cakes, and cake slackened as part of a national trend toward health consciousness. Some analysts noted that the increased consumption of cupcakes and sweet yeast raised donuts was contrary to the general trend toward more healthy products. They attributed the continuing popularity of these items to convenience.

Leading competitors in cupcakes are from large grocery stores or full-service bakeries and rely on name alone to bring in customers with little attention to customer service or product quality. Websites offering online stores that allow customers to browse for and purchase and send cupcakes, and other items via the Internet have become more commonplace as well. Our advantage in this regard is that these companies rely on preservatives in order to keep the product safe for the duration of the delivery. Our cupcakes are baked fresh daily and have a superior flavor.

Leading competitors in coffee purchase and roast high quality, whole-bean coffees and, along with Italian-style espresso beverages, cold-blended beverages, a variety of cupcakes and confections, coffee-related accessories and equipment, and a line of premium teas, sell these items primarily through company-operated retail stores. In addition to sales through company-operated retail stores, leading competitors sell coffee and tea products through other channels of distribution (specialty operations).

Coffee and cupcake shops are the fastest growing segments of the foodservice industry, and there is a pent up demand for a localized alternative to the industries dominant players.

4.4 Marketing Trends

In addition to the flood of gourmet restaurants and cooking schools that created great interest in more creative dining, supermarkets began to hone in on the competition for challenging tastes. By the late 1990s all sorts of interesting trends were occurring at the grocery store. In the fast-paced society of families that might have had both spouses and teenage children working, the need for convenience food was still crucial to successful sales in all sectors of American society.

Expensive liqueur-filled chocolate truffles and Dove ice cream bars were some gourmet items that satisfy American curiosity. By the end of the twentieth century baby food had evolved, too, into an item of gourmet proportions.

In a December 2004 article for *Fast Company* John Gilbert Dunkin Donuts marketing vice president said "Taking a look at data that indicates that Americans have become a nation of snackers, not meal-eaters. They point to the explosion of tapas menus in the trend-setting precincts of the restaurant business, and the vast appetizer menus now appearing at such national chains such as Houlihan's and The Cheesecake Factory, as the proof that the concept has legs."

Burlington is experiencing a trend toward the creation of evening dining/entertainment venues. They are popular and gaining more recognition. Evidence of this is found in local news and magazine coverage. These venues are finding new homes in the areas close to and/or adjacent to downtown.

The city's burgeoning music scene is growing and in need of more venues to accommodate the mainstream hip hop, rhythm and blues, jazz, Latin, and music artists that are choosing Burlington as home for their production efforts.

The market opportunity for gourmet cupcake/coffee shop establishments has never been better in this area of Burlington. The immediate area surrounding the business venue is undergoing a building renaissance as many residents chose to move into the city.

5.0 Strategy and Implementation Summary

The Extreme Cupcakes coffeehouse uses a strategy of total quality - in product and service. Our promise is in the products we sell, the people we attract and the atmosphere we create.

Strategic Assumptions:

People want a great-tasting cupcake

- Coffee drinkers want a more inviting coffeehouse environment
- Cupcakes and coffee drinks are considered an affordable luxury
- The coffeehouse industry is largely unaffected by the economy and world events

5.1 Competitive Edge

Our competitive edge, compared to the other cupcake/coffeehouses in the greater Burlington area includes the following:

- A significantly higher quality, better tasting product.

- Our current location in the heart of the popular downtown business district in Burlington.

189

- An ambiance superior to all other cupcake/coffeehouses in the area with upscale contemporary look. The only coffee-house downtown to provide regular weekend evening entertainment.

- A wider variety of ever changing cupcakes popular drinks than our competitors, including flavored coffee drinks, tea, chai, hot chocolate, juice and sodas.

- Our Internet website will include sales of cupcakes, tea, gift items and gift baskets.

- Extreme offers several unique advantages over all other cupcake/coffeehouses

Website
Our website is fully e-commerce functional and could easily become a significant revenue source.
We will eventually sell the following items online:

- Cupcakes (local sales/delivery only)
- Whole coffee beans, tea
- Gift baskets
- Gift items

The website also markets Extreme with:

- A monthly newsletter
- Interesting information about the cupcake and coffee industry
- A map to our store
- Store hours
- Special events
- Recipes
- Short YouTube ready videos

Trend-setters
Burlington is home to thousands of individuals who can be important to the successful positioning of Extreme Cupcakes. One mention on a TV talk program or in a 'lifestyle' magazine can (and has) launched many successful careers and businesses.

With literally hundreds of celebrities and wealthy business people as local residents, the word-of-mouth recommendations from these

190

people can drive significant business to us as well as generate favorable publicity. Many celebrities live, visit or have second homes in Vermont. Politicians and entertainers have interests in several restaurants. Celebrities in Burlington are also actively involved in the community, many supporting several local charities. Our involvement in the community will enable us to garner exposure for Extreme among an important group of local residents. Key individuals will be targeted with gift baskets from Extreme containing samples of our products to entice them to visit us and talk about us with their friends.

Design style

The interior design Extreme will be unlike any other coffeehouse chain. While there are some upscale designs, they are all of the modern Italian or Starbucks look. Our upscale stylized contemporary modern style differentiates us from all others.

Gift Items

We carry a wide variety of quality gift items, including gift baskets. Gift basket business could eventually grow to be substantial. However, since it is difficult to project at this time we have not included it in the financial computations.

Sampling

We will engage in several sampling activities to introduce potential customers (and current customers) to Extreme Cupcakes' range of drink options.

- Samples will be distributed at the restaurant
- Samples will be given to passers-by on the street
- Discount coupons will be distributed on the street, via direct mail and at special events
- Complementary cupcakes will be served at charitable and civic events
- Free cupcake service will be provided to the Chamber of Commerce, a radio station, the newspaper and at select government offices (e.g. the Planning and Zoning Department)

Portable Kiosk

Within 6 to 8 months we will create a portable Extreme kiosk to sell and market our products at special events and community activities. Burlington has many events every year. It will be an excellent way to publicize Extreme Cupcakes.
The kiosk will be highly visible and fun. It will also potentially be very profitable, although it's hard to determine how profitable with any

accuracy until the local response is measured. We believe it could generate $75,000 - $100,000 annual revenue

Pre-paid, frequency and discount cards

We will promote our program of gift cards and customer frequency cards to drive business and stimulate cash flow. Industry records indicate that 25% - 40% of all gift card amounts go unused. Also, gift cards have proven to be a popular holiday item accounting for more than 5% of total sales during December. Pre-paid cards have also proven to be very popular with the major chain cupcake and coffee shops, again accounting for a significant percentage of sales. These cards promote customer loyalty as well. Frequency cards rewarding the repeat customer with a free drink after a specified number of visits are popular and proven methods to forge customer loyalty. Discount cards are used to build goodwill among specific groups such as the Chamber of Commerce members and college students.

APPENDIX

	Sales Forecast		
	2008	2009	2010
Unit Sales			
Cupcakes	132,000	145,860	160,446
Beverages	66,000	72,930	80,223
Other	22,000	24,310	26,471
Total Unit Sales	220,000	243,100	267,140
Unit Prices	2008	2009	2010
Cupcakes	$1.25	$1.30	$1.40
Beverages	$4.00	$4.10	$4.20
Other	$5.00	$5.10	$5.20
Sales			
Cupcakes	$165,000	$189,618	$224,624
Beverages	$264,000	$299,013	$336,937
Other	$110,000	$123,981	$137,649
Total Sales	$539,000	$612,612	$699,210
Direct Unit Costs	2008	2009	2010
Cupcakes	$0.25	$0.26	$0.28
Beverages	$0.50	$0.53	$0.55
Other	$0.50	$0.53	$0.55
Direct Cost of Sales			
Cupcakes	$33,000	$38,288	$44,223
Beverages	$33,000	$38,288	$44,223
Other	$11,000	$12,884	$14,559
Subtotal Direct Cost of Sales	$77,000	$89,461	$103,005

Sales Strategy

Our sales strategy includes:

- Staff salaries that are 10% above the industry average in order to attract the best people
- Hiring for attitude so that we always have a friendly, enthusiastic staff to make customers feel welcome and appreciated; constant staff training to assure the best quality possible
- State-of-the-art sales/inventory system to (A) reduce customer waiting time, and (B) create efficient product ordering
- Create a mobile kiosk to take Extreme into the community at special events, farmer's markets, art shows, etc.
- Sell cupcakes, coffee, gift baskets and other pastries on our website
- Establish cupcake and coffee service at local businesses
- Sell gift cards, frequency cards, pre-paid cards, and offer discounts to key groups
- Create an ongoing sampling program
- Conduct a consistent, aggressive marketing program
- Be an active member of the community; be visible at charitable functions
- Solicit customer feedback to constantly improve and streamline our operation

Key Strategy: an advanced and expandable point-of-sales system

After carefully tracking the performance of the Burlington store through an expandable and highly detailed point-of-sale system, we will use this as a "blueprint" for expansion. For example, daily sales are tracked and analyzed by item, time period and cost of goods. Labor requirements are matched to projected in-store sales based upon past performance for maximum efficiency. Even after paying higher than average wages we expect to allocate no more than 25% to labor costs.

Sales are linked to inventory to both streamline the efficiency of ordering and reduce "shrinkage" by instantly alerting us to unusual shortages compared with revenues.

Scheduling can be done online and easily revised to accommodate changes - all while projecting weekly, monthly, quarterly or annual labor costs. Schedules can be sent via email to staff members.

Cost of goods can be monitored for increased efficiency too. As we continually research methods of delivering a high quality but cost-efficient product, and by making small incremental improvements in the costs of items we expect to increase overall COG by a minimum of 5% during the first year of operation.

194

APPENDIX

As expansion occurs, the POS system can be adapted to each individual location and allow the central office to monitor the stores remotely as well as the overall combined operation. Close monitoring will allow us to achieve a high level of communication between stores as well as spot problems immediately and take corrective action

6.0 Management Team

Paula Spencer has extensive experience in management and high volume production, and is a Production Supervisor for a northeast Bakery.

6.1 Personnel Plan

As the personnel plan shows, Extreme Cupcakes Inc. expects to make significant investments in sales, sales support, and product development personnel. Extreme will 2 managers, 2 pastry bakers, and 6 baristas.

7.0 Financial Plan

Extreme Cupcakes Inc. expects to raise $10,000 of its own capital, and to borrow $30,000 guaranteed by the SBA as a ten-year loan. This provides the bulk of the current financing required.

7.1 Break-even Analysis

Extreme Cupcakes' Break-even Analysis is based on the average of the first-year figures for total sales by units, and by operating expenses. These are presented as per-unit revenue, per-unit cost, and fixed costs. These conservative assumptions make for a more accurate estimate of real risk. Extreme Cupcakes should break even by the fourth month of its operation as it steadily increases its sales.

7.2 Projected Profit and Loss

As the Profit and Loss table shows, Extreme Cupcakes Incorporated expects to continue its steady growth in profitability over the next three years of operations.

Pro Forma Profit and Loss			
	2008	2009	2010
Sales	$539,000	$612,612	$699,210
Direct Costs of Goods	$77,000	$89,461	$103,005
Other	$0	$0	$0
	------------	------------	------------
Cost of Goods Sold	$77,000	$89,461	$103,005
Gross Margin	$462,000	$523,151	$596,205
Gross Margin %	85.71%	85.40%	85.27%
Expenses			
Payroll	$240,800	$253,840	$267,282
Sales and Marketing and Other Expenses	$27,000	$35,200	$71,460
Depreciation	$60,000	$69,000	$79,350
Utilities	$1,200	$1,260	$1,323
Payroll Taxes	$39,120	$41,076	$43,130
Other	$0	$0	$0
	------------	------------	------------
Total Operating Expenses	$368,120	$400,376	$462,545
Profit Before Interest and Taxes	$93,880	$122,775	$133,660
EBITDA	$153,880	$191,775	$213,010
Interest Expense	$18,100	$17,600	$16,350
Taxes Incurred	$19,261	$26,294	$29,816
Net Profit	$56,519	$78,881	$87,494
Net Profit/Sales	10.49%	12.88%	12.51%

APPENDIX

7.3 Projected Cash Flow

The cash flow projection shows that provisions for ongoing expenses are adequate to meet our needs as we generate cash flow sufficient to support the daily operation.

Pro Forma Cash Flow	2008	2009	2010
Cash Received			
Cash from Operations			
Cash Sales	$539,000	$612,612	$699,210
Subtotal Cash from Operations	$539,000	$612,612	$699,210
Additional Cash Received			
Sales Tax, VAT, HST/GST Received	$0	$0	$0
New Current Borrowing	$0	$0	$0
New Other Liabilities (interest-free)	$0	$0	$0
New Long-term Liabilities	$0	$0	$0
Sales of Other Current Assets	$0	$0	$0
Sales of Long-term Assets	$0	$0	$0
New Investment Received	$0	$0	$0
Subtotal Cash Received	$539,000	$612,612	$699,210
Expenditures	2008	2009	2010
Expenditures from Operations			
Cash Spending	$240,800	$253,840	$267,282
Bill Payments	$167,071	$208,167	$260,630
Subtotal Spent on Operations	$407,871	$462,007	$527,912
Additional Cash Spent			
Sales Tax, VAT, HST/GST Paid Out	$0	$0	$0
Principal Repayment of Current Borrowing	$0	$0	$0
Other Liabilities Principal Repayment	$0	$0	$0
Long-term Liabilities Principal Repayment	$0	$10,000	$15,000
Purchase Other Current Assets	$0	$0	$0
Purchase Long-term Assets	$0	$20,000	$20,000
Dividends	$0	$0	$0
Subtotal Cash Spent	$407,871	$492,007	$562,912
Net Cash Flow	$131,129	$120,605	$136,298
Cash Balance	$201,129	$321,734	$458,032

7.4 Balance Sheet

The following is a projected Balance Sheet for Extreme Cupcakes Incorporated.

Pro Forma Balance Sheet	2008	2009	2010
Assets			
Current Assets			
Cash	$201,129	$321,734	$458,032
Other Current Assets	$12,000	$12,000	$12,000
Total Current Assets	$213,129	$333,734	$470,032
Long-term Assets			
Long-term Assets	$65,000	$85,000	$105,000
Accumulated Depreciation	$60,000	$129,000	$208,350
Total Long-term Assets	$5,000	($44,000)	($103,350)
Total Assets	$218,129	$289,734	$366,682
Liabilities and Capital	2008	2009	2010
Current Liabilities			
Accounts Payable	$14,610	$17,333	$21,788
Current Borrowing	$0	$0	$0
Other Current Liabilities	$0	$0	$0
Subtotal Current Liabilities	$14,610	$17,333	$21,788
Long-term Liabilities	$181,000	$171,000	$156,000
Total Liabilities	$195,610	$188,333	$177,788
Paid-in Capital	$30,000	$30,000	$30,000
Retained Earnings	($64,000)	($7,481)	$71,401
Earnings	$56,519	$78,881	$87,494
Total Capital	$22,519	$101,401	$188,895
Total Liabilities and Capital	$218,129	$289,734	$366,682
Net Worth	$22,519	$101,401	$188,895

7.5 Sales Forecast

The following is a projected Sales Forecast for Extreme Cupcakes In-corporated. January - May

Sales Forecast

	Jan-08	Feb-08	Mar-08	Apr-08	May-08
Unit Sales					
Cupcakes	11,000	11,000	11,000	11,000	11,000
Beverages	5,500	5,500	5,500	5,500	5,500
Other	1,833	1,833	1,833	1,833	1,833
Total Unit Sales	18,333	18,333	18,333	18,333	18,333
Unit Prices	Jan-08	Feb-08	Mar-08	Apr-08	May-08
Cupcakes	$1.25	$1.25	$1.25	$1.25	$1.25
Beverages	$4.00	$4.00	$4.00	$4.00	$4.00
Other	$5.00	$5.00	$5.00	$5.00	$5.00
Sales					
Cupcakes	$13,750	$13,750	$13,750	$13,750	$13,750
Beverages	$22,000	$22,000	$22,000	$22,000	$22,000
Other	$9,167	$9,167	$9,167	$9,167	$9,167
Total Sales	$44,917	$44,917	$44,917	$44,917	$44,917
Direct Unit Costs	Jan-08	Feb-08	Mar-08	Apr-08	May-08
Cupcakes	$0.25	$0.25	$0.25	$0.25	$0.25
Beverages	$0.50	$0.50	$0.50	$0.50	$0.50
Other	$0.50	$0.50	$0.50	$0.50	$0.50
Direct Cost of Sales					
Cupcakes	$2,750	$2,750	$2,750	$2,750	$2,750
Beverages	$2,750	$2,750	$2,750	$2,750	$2,750
Other	$917	$917	$917	$917	$917
Subtotal Direct Cost of Sales	$6,417	$6,417	$6,417	$6,417	$6,417

Start a Cupcake Business Today

The following is a projected Sales Forecast for Extreme Cupcakes Incorporated. June - December

Sales Forecast

	Jun-08	Jul-08	Aug-08	Sep-08	Oct-08	Nov-08	Dec-08
Unit Sales							
Cupcakes	11,000	11,000	11,000	11,000	11,000	11,000	11,000
Beverages	5,500	5,500	5,500	5,500	5,500	5,500	5,500
Other	1,833	1,833	1,833	1,833	1,833	1,833	1,833
Total Unit Sales	18,333	18,333	18,333	18,333	18,333	18,333	18,333
Unit Prices	Jun-08	Jul-08	Aug-08	Sep-08	Oct-08	Nov-08	Dec-08
Cupcakes	$1.25	$1.25	$1.25	$1.25	$1.25	$1.25	$1.25
Beverages	$4.00	$4.00	$4.00	$4.00	$4.00	$4.00	$4.00
Other	$5.00	$5.00	$5.00	$5.00	$5.00	$5.00	$5.00
Sales							
Cupcakes	$13,750	$13,750	$13,750	$13,750	$13,750	$13,750	$13,750
Beverages	$22,000	$22,000	$22,000	$22,000	$22,000	$22,000	$22,000
Other	$9,167	$9,167	$9,167	$9,167	$9,167	$9,167	$9,167
Total Sales	$44,917	$44,917	$44,917	$44,917	$44,917	$44,917	$44,917
Direct Unit Costs	Jun-08	Jul-08	Aug-08	Sep-08	Oct-08	Nov-08	Dec-08
Cupcakes	$0.25	$0.25	$0.25	$0.25	$0.25	$0.25	$0.25
Beverages	$0.50	$0.50	$0.50	$0.50	$0.50	$0.50	$0.50
Other	$0.50	$0.50	$0.50	$0.50	$0.50	$0.50	$0.50
Direct Cost of Sales							
Cupcakes	$2,750	$2,750	$2,750	$2,750	$2,750	$2,750	$2,750
Beverages	$2,750	$2,750	$2,750	$2,750	$2,750	$2,750	$2,750
Other	$917	$917	$917	$917	$917	$917	$917
Subtotal Direct Cost of Sales	$6,417	$6,417	$6,417	$6,417	$6,417	$6,417	$6,417

APPENDIX

The following is a projected **Pro Forma Profit and Loss** for Extreme Cupcakes Incorporated. January – May

Pro Forma Profit and Loss January – June

	Jan-08	Feb-08	Mar-08	Apr-08	May-08	**Jun-08**
Sales	$44,917	$44,917	$44,917	$44,917	$44,917	$44,917
Direct Costs of Goods	$6,417	$6,417	$6,417	$6,417	$6,417	$6,417
Other	$0	$0	$0	$0	$0	$0
	------------	------------	------------	------------	------------	------------
Cost of Goods Sold	$6,417	$6,417	$6,417	$6,417	$6,417	$6,417
Gross Margin	$38,500	$38,500	$38,500	$38,500	$38,500	$38,500
Gross Margin %	85.71%	85.71%	85.71%	85.71%	85.71%	85.71%
Expenses						
Payroll	$20,067	$20,067	$20,067	$20,067	$20,067	$20,067
Sales and Marketing and Other Expenses	$2,250	$2,250	$2,250	$2,250	$2,250	$2,250
Depreciation	$5,000	$5,000	$5,000	$5,000	$5,000	$5,000
Utilities	$100	$100	$100	$100	$100	$100
Payroll Taxes	$3,260	$3,260	$3,260	$3,260	$3,260	$3,260
Other	$0	$0	$0	$0	$0	$0
	------------	------------	------------	------------	------------	------------
Total Operating Expenses	$30,677	$30,677	$30,677	$30,677	$30,677	$30,677
Profit Before Interest and Taxes	$7,823	$7,823	$7,823	$7,823	$7,823	$7,823
EBITDA	$12,823	$12,823	$12,823	$12,823	$12,823	$12,823
Interest Expense	$1,508	$1,508	$1,508	$1,508	$1,508	$1,508
Taxes Incurred	$1,894	$1,579	$1,579	$1,579	$1,579	$1,579
Net Profit	$4,420	$4,736	$4,736	$4,736	$4,736	$4,736
Net Profit/Sales	9.84%	10.54%	10.54%	10.54%	10.54%	10.54%

The following is a projected **Pro Forma Profit and Loss** for Extreme Cupcakes Incorporated. June – December

Pro Forma Profit and Loss July – December

	Jul-08	Aug-08	Sep-08	Oct-08	Nov-08	Dec-08
Sales	$44,917	$44,917	$44,917	$44,917	$44,917	$44,917
Direct Costs of Goods	$6,417	$6,417	$6,417	$6,417	$6,417	$6,417
Other	$0	$0	$0	$0	$0	$0
Cost of Goods Sold	$6,417	$6,417	$6,417	$6,417	$6,417	$6,417
Gross Margin	$38,500	$38,500	$38,500	$38,500	$38,500	$38,500
Gross Margin %	85.71%	85.71%	85.71%	85.71%	85.71%	85.71%
Expenses						
Payroll	$20,067	$20,067	$20,067	$20,067	$20,067	$20,067
Sales and Marketing and Other Expenses	$2,250	$2,250	$2,250	$2,250	$2,250	$2,250
Depreciation	$5,000	$5,000	$5,000	$5,000	$5,000	$5,000
Utilities	$100	$100	$100	$100	$100	$100
Payroll Taxes	$3,260	$3,260	$3,260	$3,260	$3,260	$3,260
Other	$0	$0	$0	$0	$0	$0
Total Operating Expenses	$30,677	$30,677	$30,677	$30,677	$30,677	$30,677
Profit Before Interest and Taxes	$7,823	$7,823	$7,823	$7,823	$7,823	$7,823
EBITDA	$12,823	$12,823	$12,823	$12,823	$12,823	$12,823
Interest Expense	$1,508	$1,508	$1,508	$1,508	$1,508	$1,508
Taxes Incurred	$1,579	$1,579	$1,579	$1,579	$1,579	$1,579
Net Profit	$4,736	$4,736	$4,736	$4,736	$4,736	$4,736
Net Profit/Sales	10.54%	10.54%	10.54%	10.54%	10.54%	10.54%

APPENDIX

The following is a projected **Pro Forma Balance Sheet** for Extreme Cupcakes Incorporated. January - June

Pro Forma Balance Sheet January – June 2008

		Jan-08	Feb-08	Mar-08	Apr-08	May-08	Jun-08
Assets	Starting Balances						
Current Assets							
Cash	$70,000	$94,336	$103,767	$113,503	$123,239	$132,975	$142,712
Other Current Assets	$12,000	$12,000	$12,000	$12,000	$12,000	$12,000	$12,000
Total Current Assets	$82,000	$106,336	$115,767	$125,503	$135,239	$144,975	$154,712
Long-term Assets							
Long-term Assets	$65,000	$65,000	$65,000	$65,000	$65,000	$65,000	$65,000
Accumulated Depreciation	$0	$5,000	$10,000	$15,000	$20,000	$25,000	$30,000
Total Long-term Assets	$65,000	$60,000	$55,000	$50,000	$45,000	$40,000	$35,000
Total Assets	$147,000	$166,336	$170,767	$175,503	$180,239	$184,975	$189,712
Liabilities and Capital		Jan-08	Feb-08	Mar-08	Apr-08	May-08	Jun-08
Current Liabilities							
Accounts Payable	$0	$14,915	$14,610	$14,610	$14,610	$14,610	$14,610
Current Borrowing	$0	$0	$0	$0	$0	$0	$0
Other Current Liabilities	$0	$0	$0	$0	$0	$0	$0
Subtotal Current Liabilities	$0	$14,915	$14,610	$14,610	$14,610	$14,610	$14,610
Long-term Liabilities	$181,000	$181,000	$181,000	$181,000	$181,000	$181,000	$181,000
Total Liabilities	$181,000	$195,915	$195,610	$195,610	$195,610	$195,610	$195,610
Paid-in Capital	$30,000	$30,000	$30,000	$30,000	$30,000	$30,000	$30,000
Retained Earnings	($64,000)	($64,000)	($64,000)	($64,000)	($64,000)	($64,000)	($64,000)
Earnings	$0	$4,420	$9,157	$13,893	$18,629	$23,365	$28,102
Total Capital	($34,000)	($29,580)	($24,843)	($20,107)	($15,371)	($10,635)	($5,898)
Total Liabilities and Capital	$147,000	$166,336	$170,767	$175,503	$180,239	$184,975	$189,712
Net Worth	($34,000)	($29,580)	($24,843)	($20,107)	($15,371)	($10,635)	($5,898)

The following is a projected **Pro Forma Balance Sheet** for Extreme Cupcakes Incorporated. July– December

Pro Forma Balance Sheet July– December 2008

Assets	Starting Balances	Jul-08	Aug-08	Sep-08	Oct-08	Nov-08	Dec-08
Current Assets							
Cash	$70,000	$152,448	$162,184	$171,920	$181,657	$191,393	$201,129
Other Current Assets	$12,000	$12,000	$12,000	$12,000	$12,000	$12,000	$12,000
Total Current Assets	$82,000	$164,448	$174,184	$183,920	$193,657	$203,393	$213,129
Long-term Assets							
Long-term Assets	$65,000	$65,000	$65,000	$65,000	$65,000	$65,000	$65,000
Accumulated Depreciation	$0	$35,000	$40,000	$45,000	$50,000	$55,000	$60,000
Total Long-term Assets	$65,000	$30,000	$25,000	$20,000	$15,000	$10,000	$5,000
Total Assets	$147,000	$194,448	$199,184	$203,920	$208,657	$213,393	$218,129
Liabilities and Capital		Jul-08	Aug-08	Sep-08	Oct-08	Nov-08	Dec-08
Current Liabilities							
Accounts Payable	$0	$14,610	$14,610	$14,610	$14,610	$14,610	$14,610
Current Borrowing	$0	$0	$0	$0	$0	$0	$0
Other Current Liabilities	$0	$0	$0	$0	$0	$0	$0
Subtotal Current Liabilities	$0	$14,610	$14,610	$14,610	$14,610	$14,610	$14,610
Long-term Liabilities	$181,000	$181,000	$181,000	$181,000	$181,000	$181,000	$181,000
Total Liabilities	$181,000	$195,610	$195,610	$195,610	$195,610	$195,610	$195,610
Paid-in Capital	$30,000	$30,000	$30,000	$30,000	$30,000	$30,000	$30,000
Retained Earnings	($64,000)	($64,000)	($64,000)	($64,000)	($64,000)	($64,000)	($64,000)
Earnings	$0	$32,838	$37,574	$42,310	$47,047	$51,783	$56,519
Total Capital	($34,000)	($1,162)	$3,574	$8,310	$13,047	$17,783	$22,519
Total Liabilities and Capital	$147,000	$194,448	$199,184	$203,920	$208,657	$213,393	$218,129
Net Worth	($34,000)	($1,162)	$3,574	$8,311	$13,047	$17,783	$22,519

EDUCATION RESOURCES

Culinary Schools with a Baking Emphasis

American Institute of Baking (AIB)
AIB is a not-for-profit corporation, founded by the North American wholesale and retail baking industries in 1919 as a technology transfer center for food processors and bakers.

Ballymaloe Cookery School, Ireland
Founded in 1983, Ballymaloe is one of Europe's foremost cookery schools. Unlike any other cookery school in the world the school is located in the middle of a 100-acre, organic farm of which ten acres are devoted to organic market gardens, orchards and greenhouses.

The Culinary Institute of America (CIA)
The CIA offers associate and bachelor's degree programs in Culinary Arts and Baking and Pastry Arts. Also, Continuing Education for foodservice professionals is offered both in Hyde Park, NY and St. Helena, CA.

The French Culinary Institute
The French Culinary Institute offers day and evening programs in Classic Culinary Arts, Classic Pastry Arts as well as short Courses for the Serious Amateur and Short Pastry Courses.

Johnson and Wales University
The College of Culinary Arts offers a variety of programs for students, professionals and food enthusiasts. Degree programs are offered in both the day school and in Continuing Education in the evenings and on weekends. Main campus located in Providence, RI. Other campuses include Charlotte, NC; North Miami, FL; and Denver, CO

International School of Baking
Based upon the premise that fewer is better, the International School of Baking, located in Bend, Oregon, teaches rigorous classes to one or two students who work in a hands-on environment with the instructor.

Kendall College
Founded in 1984, The School of Culinary Arts and Hotel Restaurant management at Kendall College is considered one of the leading culinary schools in the country. Students complete an intensive, sequentially organized curriculum under the direction of certified chef-instructors.

Texas Culinary Academy
Le Cordon Bleu's world-renowned culinary training in Austin, Texas offers AAS Degrees in Culinary Arts and Hospitality and Restaurant Management and a certificate in Patisserie and Baking.

San Francisco Baking Institute
Classes and seminars provide a strong foundation of Artisan Baking skills, an overall appreciation of baking and pastry arts and the opportunity to flourish creatively in small, hands-on classes. Programs benefit professional bakers wishing to refine skills and techniques, bakery owners who recognize the importance of well trained staff and baking enthusiasts looking to change careers and open a bakery or just have fun with serious home baking.

Professional Organizations
These organizations will be very valuable in terms of your business plan industry research. While you may not refer to these organizations very often, they can provide an invaluable service as a professional knowledge center.

American Society of Baking
http://www.asbe.org/
The American Society of Baking, formerly known as the American Society of Bakery Engineers, is a professional society comprised of members who are either engaged in, involved with, or interested in wholesale or large-scale bakery production.

AIB International
www.aibonline.org
AIB International's mission is to "put science to work for the baker," AIB's staff includes experts in the fields of baking production; research related to experimental baking, cereal science, and nutrition; food safety and hygiene; occupational safety; and maintenance engineering.

American Culinary Federation (ACF)
The American Culinary Federation, Inc. is a professional, not-for-profit organization for chefs. The principal goal of the founding chefs remains true today - to promote a professional image of the American chef worldwide through education among culinarians at all levels.

International Cake Exploration Societé
ICES is an organization of over 4,000 members worldwide. Its members share one thing -a love of sugar crafting. They create works of confectionery art with buttercream, gumpaste, pastillage, fondant and many other edible media. The site has information about chapters, recipes, scholarships, decorating events and links.

Retailer's Bakery Association (RBA)

www.rbanet.com

A trade association creating industry-specific training programs, developing profit tools and connecting retailers with suppliers and industry experts.

Trade Publications

American Cake Decorating Magazine
http://www.americancakedecorating.com/

Bakingbusiness.com
Publishers of three industry publications covering aspects of the baking industry, *Baking Buyer, Milling and Baking News, and Baking and Snack*

Baking Buyer
Specializes in reporting on industry news, new product trends and merchandising ideas for executives and entrepreneurs managing retail, in store, foodservice and niche wholesale bakeries. Each issue features the industry's leading operations, highlights innovative marketing and product ideas, and showcases the latest equipment, ingredients, supplies, and services

BakeryNet
http://bakery-net.com/
A storehouse of bakery information for the bakery industry professional, from the publishers of *Modern Baking and Baking Management.*

Modern Baking
http://modern-baking.com/
Modern Baking is the retail bakery foods industry's most-read journal.

Baking Management
http://baking-management.com/
Baking Management brings volume bakery managers the information they need to stay in front. While geared toward large operations, small businesses can still take advantage of the consumer research and trends.

Internet Community Resources
Bake Space
www.bakespace.com/forums/index.php

Bakery-Net
www.bakery-net.com
Everything for the baker: buyer's guide, company listing,
associations, industry news, want ads, schools
Bakery-Net Forums
http://forums.bakery-net.com/index.php

Chef Talk Baking Forum
http://tinyurl.com/cupcake6

Chef Talk Professional Pastry Chef Forum
http://tinyurl.com/cupcake7

King Arthur Flour's Online Baking Classes
http://tinyurl.com/cupcake8

Top Tastes Forum: Desserts and Baking
http://tinyurl.com/cupcake9

Internet: Flour and Ingredients
Cook Natural Products
http://www.cooknaturally.com

General Mills
http://www.generalmills.com

King Arthur Flour
http://www.kingarthurflour.com

Lake County Walnuts
http://www.lcwalnut.com

Lesaffre
http://www.lesaffre.fr

Plugrá Butter
http://www.butter1.com

Business Resources

International Dairy-Deli-Bakery Association
www.iddba.org
Information on IDDBA membership, products and services, podcasts, annual expo and seminar, links to other food sites.

American Bakers Association
www.americanbakers.org

This organization deals with legislative issues concerning bakery industry.

Food Marketing Institute
www.fmi.org

Information on FMI membership, events, publications, industry & consumer matters, press releases.

Bakery Equipment Manufacturers Association
Equipment suppliers
www.bema.org

Small Business Administration
www.sba.gov
Online resource for small business information and publications.

Cupcake Specific Resources
There are so many independent blogs now that they could take up an entire chapter to list. These are just a few of our favorites:

CakeCentral
http://www.cakecentral.com
Largest Cake Decorating community. Recipes, Photos, Instruction

Cupcakes Take the Cake
http://cupcakestakethecake.blogspot.com/ -- Everything Cupcakes: Reviews, articles, news, interviews

Cupcake Pictures
Cupcake photography community. See and cupcakes out in the wild. Incredible artistry

Cake Journal
http://www.cakejournal.com
Cake Decorating blog with many how-to's

CakeSpy
http://www.cakespy.com/ Articles and reviews

The Cake Lab
http://thecakelab.com/blog-- How-to's and tutorials

Bakerella
http://www.bakerella.blogspot.com/ --Famous for her Cupcake pops, featured on Martha Stewart

U.S. GUIDELINES FOR BAKERIES

Alabama
Public Health Dept. Mark Sestak 334-206-5375
http://www.adph.org/
All permitting and inspections handled at county level
Business License: at county level:
http://tinyurl.com/cupcakeAL1

Alaska
Alaska Department of Environmental Conservation, Division of Environmental Health, Food Safety and Sanitation Program; Kim Stryker (907) 269-7501.
Submit plan for approval: **http://tinyurl.com/cupcakeAK2**
Apply for a permit: **http://tinyurl.com/cupcakeAK3**
State will then inspect and issue permit if everything is approved.
Business License:
http://tinyurl.com/cupcakeAK4

Arizona
Per Arizona Department of Health, (602) 542-1023. Everything handled at county level.

Arkansas
Food Plan Review Guidelines
http://tinyurl.com/cupcakeAK1
Guidelines for food establishments
http://tinyurl.com/cupcakeAK

California
Processed food registration (916) 558-1784
Must contact local health department for licensing and inspection. Business license is handled locally.

Colorado
http://tinyurl.com/cupcakeCO1
Dan Rifkin State Public Health Dept. 303-692-3644

http://www.cdphe.state.co.us/
All permitting and inspections handled through county.
Must obtain Sales tax license from the state.
Info and application: **http://tinyurl.com/cupcakeCO2**

Connecticut
http://tinyurl.com/cupcakeCT
Dept of Consumer Protection, 860-713-6160
Subject to state and local zoning and health laws. State requires plan review and license application followed by state inspection. Business license registered with town clerk.

DC
http://tinyurl.com/cupcakeDC
Office of Consumer and Regulatory Affairs, 202-442-4576

Delaware
http://tinyurl.com/cupcakeDE
Business license: **http://tinyurl.com/cupcakeDE2**

Florida
Must have site plans approved,
http://tinyurl.com/cupcakeFL1
Permit application: **http://tinyurl.com/cupcakeFL2**
Business licenses from City or County Occupational License Department.

Georgia
Dept. Of Agriculture (404) 656-3621 Mark Norton, mnorton@agr.state.ga.us
http://tinyurl.com/cupcakeGA1
Actual applications and permits issued through county but inspections by state. Business license from city/county.

Hawaii

Start a Cupcake Business Today

Must submit plan for review:
Oahu: **http://tinyurl.com/cupcakeHI**
Hilo: **http://tinyurl.com/cupcakeHI**
Kona; **http://tinyurl.com/cupcakeHI**
Maui: **http://tinyurl.com/cupcakeHI**
Molokai: **http://tinyurl.com/cupcakeHI**
Kauai: **http://tinyurl.com/cupcakeHI**

Apply for permit:
Oahu: **http://tinyurl.com/cupcakeHI1**
Hilo: **http://tinyurl.com/cupcakeHI2**
Kona: **http://tinyurl.com/cupcakeHI2**
Maui: **http://tinyurl.com/cupcakeHI2**
Molokai: **http://tinyurl.com/cupcakeHI2**
Kauai: **http://tinyurl.com/cupcakeHI2**
Business license: **http://tinyurl.com/HIbiz1**
Create an account and then log in. Choose quickfile, Form
BB1 General Excise. Fee $22.50

Idaho
http://tinyurl.com/cupcakeID1
Environmental Health, 208-327-7499
License application: **http://tinyurl.com/cupcakeID2**
Facility requirements: **http://tinyurl.com/cupcakeID3**
Plan review and approval form:
http://www.cdhd.idaho.gov/EH/food/inspect.cfm
Assumed business name must be registered:
Instructions: **http://tinyurl.com/cupcakeID4**
Form: **http://tinyurl.com/cupcakeID5**

Illinois
http://tinyurl.com/cupcakeIL4
Elizabeth Watkins, 217-782-4977
Facility regulations:
http://www.idph.state.il.us
State considers this a food manufacturer, no licensing requirement at this time. Still subject to inspection. Must

report activity to Food Processing Coordinator 217-785-2439. Business license at county level

Indiana
http://tinyurl.com/cupcakeIN1
Department of Health, 317-439-9662
Plan review form **http://tinyurl.com/cupcakeIN2**
Application for food service
http://tinyurl.com/cupcakeIN3
Business license: No state filing required for sole proprietorships

Iowa
http://tinyurl.com/cupcakeIA1
Iowa Department of Inspections and Appeals, Food & Consumer Safety Bureau, Judy Harrison, 515/281-8587.
Mary Roaden, Mary.Roaden@dia.iowa.gov
Rules regulations and application are bundled together in download.
No other license required

Kansas
Dept. of Agriculture: Steve Moris 785-296-7430, smoris@KDA.STATE.KS.U.S.
Health Inspector: Katherine Robnut 785-207-1288

Kentucky
Cabinet for Health and Family Services, Mark Reed (502) 564-7181, Mark.Reed@ky.gov
Business license: must register with the Department of Revenue, **http://preview.tinyurl.com/cupcakeKY2** as well as obtain a local business license.

Louisiana
Louisiana Dept. of Health, Food and Drug Division. Brian Warren, (225) 342-7517, bwarren2@dhh.la.gov

http://tinyurl.com/cupcakeLA2
Bakery specific regulations:
http://tinyurl.com/cupcakeLA5
Must have plans reviewed:
http://tinyurl.com/cupcakeLA3
Step by step instructions: **http://tinyurl.com/cupcakeLA4**
Must obtain revenue account number for sales tax:
http://tinyurl.com/cupcakeLA

Maine
Dept of Agriculture , 207-287-3841, Michelle
Application: **http://tinyurl.com/cupcakeMne**
Business license issued through city/town

Maryland
http://tinyurl.com/cupcakeMD1
Maryland Department of Health, Food Division 410-767-8400 Bakery and Kitchens regulated at the county level. State only regulates food processing plants. Business license at county level. Must register trade name with state:
http://preview.tinyurl.com/cupcakeMD2

Massachusetts
http://tinyurl.com/bakeryMA
License application: **http://tinyurl.com/cupcakeMA1**
Business license issued by local government

Michigan
Dept. of Agriculture. Food and Dairy Administration. Suzanne Kidder Rick, kidders@michigan.gov, 616-356-0609, mda-info@michigan.gov
License application: **http://tinyurl.com/cupcakeMich1**
License and inspection handled at the regional level, following link shows regions and links to get to their offices:
http://tinyurl.com/cupcakeMich2
Need a Sales Tax License: Department of Treasury (517) 636-4660 and request a 518 sales tax form.

http://preview.tinyurl.com/cupcakeMich3

Minnesota
Dept of Agriculture, Food Division, 651-201-6027, Ask for Rick.
Facility requirements: **http://tinyurl.com/cupcakeMN1**
Plan review application: **http://tinyurl.com/cupcakeMN2**
Food Service Certification:
http://tinyurl.com/cupcakeMN3
Food Handlers' Licence: **http://tinyurl.com/cupcakeMN4**

Mississippi
Dept. of Health
http://tinyurl.com/cupcakeMI
Regulations: **http://tinyurl.com/cupcakeMI2**
Procedure flowchart: **http://tinyurl.com/cupcakeMI3**
Permit application: **http://tinyurl.com/cupcakeMI4**
No separate state business license required.

Missouri
Department of Health.
http://tinyurl.com/cupcakeMO
inspections and licensing handled at county/local level.
Missouri food code: **http://tinyurl.com/cupcakeMO2**
Must register fictitious business names' with the state.
FAQ about registering: **http://tinyurl.com/cupcakeMO3**
Contact information to request assistance: (573) 751-4153, 1-866-223-6535

Montana
Dept. of Public Health, Food and Consumer Safety (406) 444-4735 (Barb)
Requirements of facility, Montana rules, site plan approval: **http://tinyurl.com/cupcakeMT**
DPH issues license after inspection.

Nebraska
Department of Agriculture, Bureau of Dairies and Foods, (402) 471-2536
Licensing handled by regional inspectors and regulations differ.
General guidelines:
http://preview.tinyurl.com/cupcakeNB1
If outside Douglas and/or Lancaster County, 402-471-2536
If inside Douglas, (402) 444-7480
If inside Lancaster County, (402) 441-6280

Nevada
Department of Health, 775-684-4200, Nancy Martin
Bureau of Health Protections, Environmental Health Chad Weston 775-687-7539
Food establishment rules:
http://preview.tinyurl.com/cupcakeNV1
Plan review instructions: **http://tinyurl.com/cupcakeNV2**
Local Business license if sole proprietorship

New Hampshire
Rules: **http://tinyurl.com/cupcakeNH**
License application:
http://preview.tinyurl.com/cupcakeNH2

New Jersey
http://tinyurl.com/cupcakeNJ
Dept of Health, 609-588-3123.
Retail food businesses — such as bakeries, food stores, mobile food units, catering operations, farmers' markets, online sales, and temporary food events — are inspected and licensed by the local/municipal health department.
For more information, contact your local health department. Visit the Office of Public Health Infrastructure online (http://www.state.nj.us/health/lh/) and click on the map for a roster of local health offices and contact information.

Regulations: **http://preview.tinyurl.com/cupcakeNJ1**
Wholesale license application:
http://tinyurl.com/cupcakeNJ2
Business license: No state license for retail.

New Mexico
Must submit plans for approval.
Application for plan review:
http://tinyurl.com/cupcakeNM
Application for food permit:
http://tinyurl.com/cupcakeNM

New York
http://tinyurl.com/cupcakeNY2
Dept of Agriculture.
Must be licensed.
License application: **http://tinyurl.com/cupcakeNY**
Business license issued at county level
Regulations: **http://tinyurl.com/cupcakeNY1**

North Carolina
Food Business Assistance Program
http://tinyurl.com/cupcakeNC
Home business Guidelines:
http://tinyurl.com/cupcakeNC2
Must register with Dept of Revenue:
http://www.dornc.com/electronic/registration/checklist.html

North Dakota
http://tinyurl.com/cupcakeND1
Dept of Health, Division of Food and Lodging. Kenan Bullinger, Director - kbulling@nd.gov 701-328-1291.
Regulations: **http://tinyurl.com/cupcakeND**
Contact Food Division, 701-328-1291 for Plan review checklist. If plan approved, they will do an inspection followed by a license application.

Ohio
http://www.agri.ohio.gov/foodsafety/
Ohio Dept. of Agriculture, Division of Food Safety, 8995
East Main Street, Reynoldsburg, OH 43068. Phone: (614)
728-6250, foodsafety@agri.ohio.gov.
Regulations: **http://tinyurl.com/cupcakeOH**

Oklahoma
http://www.ok.gov/health/
Dept of Health. (405) 271-5243
Licensing and inspections at county level.
Rules: **http://tinyurl.com/cupcakeOK**
Business license: **http://tinyurl.com/OKbusiness**

Oregon
http://www.oregon.gov/ODA/FSD/
A plan review is required, **http://tinyurl.com/cupcakeOR**.
They will then conduct an inspection. If the plan and inspection are approved, then an application will be
completed at time of license issuance. Business license
must be obtained at the county level.

Pennsylvania
Dept of Agriculture
Applicant letter: **http://tinyurl.com/cupcakePA1**
Plan review guidelines: **http://tinyurl.com/cupcakePA2**
Plan review application: **http://tinyurl.com/cupcakePA3**
Business license: **http://tinyurl.com/bizPENN**

Rhode Island
http://tinyurl.com/cupcakeRI
Dept. of Health, Office of Food Protection. Ernest Julian
(401) 222-2749

South Carolina
Dept of Health and Environmental Control, Food Protection 803-896-0640.
Regulations: **http://tinyurl.com/cupcakeSC1**
Contact local Environmental Health office for permit application, fee $60.
Business license link: **http://tinyurl.com/SCbiz**

South Dakota
Dept of Health, 605-773-3361
Food service code: **http://tinyurl.com/cupcakeSD1**
Application: **http://tinyurl.com/cupcakeSD2**
Plan review questionnaire: **http://tinyurl.com/cupcakeSD3**
Guidelines: **http://tinyurl.com/cupcakeSD4**
Step by step instructions:
http://preview.tinyurl.com/cupcakeSD
Business license: contact Department of Revenue and Regulations 605-773-3311

Tennessee
http://tinyurl.com/cupcakeTN
Dept of Agriculture, Regulatory Services, Food and Dairy
http://tinyurl.com/cupcakeTN1

Texas
http://tinyurl.com/cupcakesTX
Dept of State Health Services, Food and Drug Licensing.
Rhonda Henry, (512) 834-6626 x2490.
Many cities and counties have local regulations; if so, they must be followed. If no local regulations exist, then the state licensing is followed. Contact Food and Drug Licensing Department, (512) 834-6626 for correct and up-to-date information. Due to the number of localities and the frequency of rule changes it will be the only place to get accurate updated information.

Utah
Dept of Agriculture and Foods. 801-860-7075. Rebecca Nielson
Food processing authorities:
http://tinyurl.com/cupcakesUT4
One-stop licensing and registration for business license:
http://tinyurl.com/UTbiz

Vermont
http://tinyurl.com/cupcakeVT
Dept of Health.
License application:
http://tinyurl.com/cupcakeVT1
Business license may also be required from county.

Virginia
http://www.vdacs.virginia.gov/
Department of Agriculture and Consumer Services.
(804)786-3520

Washington
Dept. of Agriculture(360) 902-1876, Lucy (360) 273-6777
Information regarding facility requirements:
http://agr.wa.gov/FoodAnimal/FoodProcessors/
Agriculture "green book", contains some information that may be useful:
http://tinyurl.com/cupcakeWA3
Hardcopies of all handbooks and forms available by calling (360) 902-1876 and requesting "food processors packet."
Business licensing guide: call (360) 664-1400 or
http://tinyurl.com/cucpakeWA4

West Virginia
http://tinyurl.com/cupcakeWV
Inspection and permitting of food establishments are the responsibility of the local health department.

Business registration packet:
http://tinyurl.com/cupcakeWV2

Wisconsin
http://tinyurl.com/cupcakeWI
All license information found here including where to re-quest application packet.

Wyoming
http://tinyurl.com/cupcakeWY
Dept of Agriculture, Consumer Protection. Linda Stratton (307) 777-6592
Facility requirements: Business license at county level
Must submit license application, plan review, and have inspection; all done through local government. Agency dependent on locality.

Visit www.cupcake-business.com/resources to download all business files and supporting documents for starting a cupcake business.

Made in the USA
Lexington, KY
24 May 2012